Praise for *Creekwater Mansions*

There is no one else rendering poetry like Ian Hall. His poems are gnarly gardens of deep appreciation of what this tangled, earthly world offers. Nouns often set loose in verbiage. And verbs set down roots in the lush soil of memory. I consider most of Hall's poems as praise poems, praise for this story we have found ourselves in, generations after a story was passed down of first man and first woman thrust from a garden for being hungry and curious. We are in it now, and Hall's potent poems illuminate the unsung details of a family, a community striving to live where to make a life is impossible.

— JOY HARJO, 23rd U.S. Poet Laureate

All too often, the contemporary poetry that gets most lauded is little more than chopped-up prose with the right attitudes, so reading Ian Hall's poems is a much-needed reminder of how the best poetry does so much more. The poems in *Creekwater Mansions* are big-hearted but never sentimental, always true to their time and place. Nevertheless, what I admire most is the sheer *aliveness* of the language, the unanticipated words or similes that reward multiple readings. I doubt a better debut book of poetry will be published this year.

— RON RASH, author of *Serena* and *The Risen*

Creekwater Mansions is wry and wise and smart-as-hell. If Tyler Childers could have studied under Robert Penn Warren, if James Still could have fallen in love with Nick Offerman, then *maybe* someone else could have written this book. As it stands, only the erudite mud dauber Ian Hall could have given us a debut so masculo-mythic, it ruins grit lit. Hear ye, hear ye: Hall is an indispensable new writer of Appalachia.

— REBECCA GAYLE HOWELL, author of *American Purgatory*

Prepare yourself for a transporting journey into the Appalachian South with all its beauty and decay, its radiance and self-destructive tendencies. The portraits of family members, friends, and assorted locals are especially rich and haunting, rendered with incredible depth, dimension, and feeling. Ian Hall has the ear and timing of a jazz master and the daring of a successful transporter of moonshine. There's hardly a line without something to admire, some moment I know I'll want to revisit in this memorable and masterful debut.

— JAMES KIMBRELL, author of *The Law of Truly Large Numbers*

CREEKWATER MANSIONS

poems

Ian Hall

Creekwater Mansions
Ian Hall

© 2026
All Rights Reserved

POETRY

ISBN   978-1-958094-66-2

Book Design: EK Larken
Cover Design: James McNulty

No part of this book may be reproduced in any way whatsoever
without written permission from the publisher,
except for brief quotations embodied in critical articles or reviews.

EastOver Press encourages the use of our publications
in educational settings. For questions about educational discounts,
contact us online: www.EastOverPress.com or info@EastOverPress.com.

PUBLISHED IN THE UNITED STATES OF AMERICA BY

EastOver Press
Rochester, Massachusetts
www.EastOverPress.com

For my late father, Charles David Hall.

You taught me everything I know about the fine art of porch-sitting.

CREEKWATER MANSIONS

Contents

Foreword   11

I

Recoil	17
Nocturne For August, Ailing Things	19
Otherlight	21
Bellyaching	23
Aesthete	25
Pilgrim	28
Local Delicacy	31
After Breakfast, Knott County, 2007	32
Hormonal	33
Parts & Labor	35
Pure Fool	37
Rite	39
If I Know Me	42
Nightwatchmen	44
Crowfare	46
Love in the Time of Company Towns	49
Visiting the Barn the Night Before I Burn it Down	52

II

Zeitgeist & Gristle	57
Sleep Apnea	59
Say Wise Things or Die, Egghead	62
Pitching Fits	65
Sons of Perdition, KY	67
Crowbarring into a Schoolhouse at an Obscene Hour	70
Diatribe of the Runner-Up in a Piddling Local Election	72
Every Day is Like Sunday	74
37.4029° N, 82.8063° W	76
Codependents	78

Injury to Insult	81
The Hay Sufferer	82
The Coalblacked Jacobins	85
A Country Horse-Doctor	87
An Undeclared Farmer, Middle Creek, Kentucky, 1862	90
Rough Customer	93
Pastoral vs. Georgic	96
The Selected Works of Judas Iscariot	98
Present Tense Timeless	101
All Assurances, This Was South	104
A Day Laborer Dreams Away His Drive Home	106
Sonnet for the Preachiest Loop in My Belt	108
We Still Kill the Old Way	109

III

The Redneckery	113
We Were Put on This Earth to Fart Around	115
Elegy for JOANN Fabrics	117
Lastward	119
Psalm to Be Spoken in a Hill's Ribcage, Where the Heart Ought Be	122
Blue Yodel for Back When	124
Those Old Chromosomes Were Known to Ramble	126
Swiftly Tilting Planet	129
Cost of Living	130
Thanks-Giving	132

Acknowledgments	*135*
Personal Thanks	*137*
About the Author	*139*

Foreword

Ian Hall has an ear and a nose for both levity and heartbreak, and for the special unsentimental melancholy that emerges when these two are combined. His debut collection of poems, *Creekwater Mansions*, announces the arrival of a fully formed vision. Many literary voices play in the background of these poems, but none rise so clearly to surface as to say it makes a clear influence or predecessor. Maybe Larry Levis, the bard of ruined California vineyards and the widening spell of the closing up of the Twentieth Century, but even Levis may not have seen how to make poetry, much less mansions of the imagination, out of the flood-or-drought creekbeds of modern Appalachia. Maurice Manning, another native-genius Kentucky poet, comes to mind with his singular blend of reverence and reverie. The originality of Hall's poetry makes itself felt and known as the reader tries to determine which of these poems are comedies and which are tragedies, and the slow realization of how pointless it can feel to try defining them as opposites. John Keats elucidated for us that "Ay, in the very temple of Delight/ Veil'd Melancholy has her sovran shrine," and Hall's rare gift is to make Delight and Melancholy sing together.

However much a specific sense of place dominates the imagery of *Creekwater Mansions*, the language is the centerpiece of this book, rich and lyrical, always searching and inventive. The opening lines from "Otherlight" show some of the virtuosity at work, using the poet's triumvirate of Diction, Tone, and Voice, each to full effect:

What's between you & time
but a bail-bondsman? Reads the flyer
tacked to the bulletin
at the Baptist Church. I'vent got anything

sage to say to that.

The speaker of the poem knows layered language when he sees it, and recognizes a larger implication in the bail bonds flyer than may be intended. Time is a prominent figure all throughout these poems, operating beyond our control and with seemingly nothing between us and it. The apostrophe usage in the compound "I'vent," a beautifully colloquial spoken rendering of "I haven't," mirrors the literary trope of apostrophe, highlighting what is missing, which will always be time. The rest of the poem meditates on the shrewd and crafty life of a grandmother after she has been widowed—"She had a candle/complexion" the speaker says—and how she managed to evade her own passing, making Death "scratch his head for a spell."

Hall practices a rare art of combination, of threading together unlikely correspondences between unlike things. One such example can be found in the opening lines of "Nocturne for August, Ailing Things":

In cadence there is the COPD
   of porch swings.
& somewhere not terribly distant the sleep
   crusted voice of an engine, steam

tapeworming off hot blacktop,
   all hauntological, after an evening
that was something to be seen

through stout glass. But, in this yard,
   between the slop-giddy hogs & sporting dogs
there is détente—a torrential hush.

In addition to bearing witness to real lives lived in Appalachian Kentucky hollers, these poems also take their readers on an intellectual trip. Reading *Creekwater Mansions* is like spending an afternoon in a great university library, where the books and writers one has only heard about are there to be discovered. Hall wears his learning lightly, where in one stanza you might encounter Jacques Derrida's intricate concept of hauntology, and in the next stanza run across "slop-giddy hogs & sporting dogs." This playfulness enlarges both the earthy and the ethereal, insisting that these two worlds belong together which have been too much divided, and that one person can meaningfully experience both the farmyard and the library.

Hilarious moments abound in this book, indicated from Mark Twain's wistful looking back on childhood in the opening epigraph, a real sense of levity in the face of boundless hardship and doing without. In "Pilgrim," the speaker describes his ascetic, saintly, and comically kind mother, a hard-bitten school-teacher from Ohio living out her life in eastern Kentucky:

.... Jolting along primly in a Lumina
with no hubcaps, she began to care for this place, its collective

mullet. Haired-over, untucked, rode hard & put up wet, she solaced them all—thirty years & counting in the classroom.

Every detail of this description, and the whole poem, makes me laugh, and also smile with recognition of my own life and my own home community. I even drove a hand-me-down Chevy Lumina for a few years in college, not to mention the mullets, mine and my friends. Even funnier is the drunken ribald telling the story of "Rite" and the gluttonous fridge-raiding of "If I Know Me," which ends "I've never been able to get enough/of too much." This is poetry for a strong stomach and a sharp, tolerant wit. I laughed out loud when I came to the line, "You & me, your curls tasseling out/ like a 4-H project," and this kept happening all through the book. So many cultural depictions of Appalachia show only the dire and downtrodden but miss the sense of humor that permeates every holler I have spent time in, and that hilarity comes fully to life in Hall's poetry.

At its heart, though, this is a book of elegies, for fathers and grandfathers, and for the lost times and faraway places of childhood. The many and varied speakers of these poems will occasionally let the truth of their sorrows slip in between tall tales, and sometimes there is a longing for someone who turned tail and ran out on their childhood, or more often someone who simply passed on too soon. There are subtle revelations of economic disparity, wherein Derrida's "Spectres of Marx" become visible in the real world of modern Appalachia, and that too is a form of elegy, as much for the lost futures of a place as for its abused past. Without overtly venturing into politics, Hall catches both the gristle and the zeitgeist, understanding and revealing something of the moment and how we got here. I would be surprised to read a better debut collection this year than *Creekwater Mansions,* though I would welcome seeing any that were nearly as good. We need all the brilliant young poets we can get these days, and I feel certain that this book marks Ian Hall's emergence as one of America's best poets in the years ahead.

—Jesse Graves
Johnson City, Tennessee

I

"May God bless my people, my uncle, my aunt, my mother, my good father, oh, remember them kindly in their time of trouble; and in the hour of their taking away.

After a little I am taken in and put to bed. Sleep, soft smiling, draws me unto her: and those receive me, who quietly treat me, as one familiar and well-beloved in that home: but will not, oh, will not, not now, not ever; but will not ever tell me who I am."
—James Agee

"To look back on one's childhood is to get the cloudy sense of having been a prince, once, in some enchanted far-off land, & of being in exile now, & desolate."
—Mark Twain

Recoil

My grandfather had an over-under
he called *Pardon Me*. It'd rip

through near anything neat
as the inaugural bite

from an apple. He let me shoot it
when I was six, & it tendered my shoulder

to mince. My father wrung his hands
every time pap let me go

bare-soled through the freshly shuffled
loam of his garden. *He'll come home*

all wormy, he said. & fretted as well
mornings we spent seining crawdads

in the brisk gray ribbon
of creek. *All you do is mouth*

pap would say
when he'd indulged enough

of his jitters. They were always
roostering. But now I'm ten, & pap

is dead. He's been in that shape
for months. His heart

brittled. There are other words
for what happened to him, but they don't

mean an iota to me. As a child, I can only stand
to know here & now. We are thrifting

through his closet, my father
& me, & I feel empty

headed from the sensuous particulars
of penny loafer, old plaid

& herringbone. We sort a while, the handsome
clothes all starched together

in clean untend. Only the white t-shirts, faint
& threadbare, have had any use. *He didn't*

*wear a one of these nice outfits
did he.* I say this & already don't know

if I regret it. The spoiled quiet. Still
my father busies himself. His fingers

spider over every garment—fold,
pleat, crease—with a washerwoman's

meek fidelity. In this vinegared hush, my stomach
trebles. I go to the toilet, deep

unclench. After a time, I rinse off, pad
feebly into the towel closet & through a distend

in the wallpapering, I watch my father
in the other room. He has one of pap's old workshirts

pressed against his face
like smelling salts.

Nocturne for August, Ailing Things

In cadence there is the COPD
        of porch swings. & somewhere
not terribly distant the sleep
        crusted voice of an engine, steam

tapeworming off hot blacktop,
        all hauntological, after an evening
that was something to be seen

through stout glass. But, in this yard,
        between the slop-giddy hogs & sporting dogs
there is détente—a torrential hush. If you could
        parse past the waxpaper of tonight, you'd see

only eyesore: the toothed spearmint
        of Camino hoods, trucks tucked
in the dust of last decade.

Jumper cables like macabre spaghetti,
        pistons, schismed manifolds: a Gettysburg
of tinker & shrapnel to paw through. But this junkage,
        this totaled zip code, does not trouble

the squirrels, who are like clockwork
        laying next season's supper away in the dark
escrow of tree holes, a clobbered sedan.
        & the locals don't bemoan it either. Breeze

grieves the shutters, shorts the circuits,
        but their rest is bassinet-pure. Heads on pillows
full of what the crummiest roosters have shed.
        & even the children so colicky

to be back at play, to again summit
        the jungle-gyms they've made

of hulled out septic tanks, have been smoothed
        moot by Nyquil

& a few sugar spoons of Rye. & a pair
        of twentysomethings are deep in the woods
of one another, still undoing buttons
        on the black flannel that midnight has spread

flat for them. Afterward, they'll shower together,
        won't even wince at the hot water heater sighing
cold curter than the word of God in the Hebrew verse,
        just fall straightway to snoring still toweled,

guts jungly from too much beer
        & cellophaned snackcake. Box fans
rasp oomphless. Bugs suicide in citronella.
        This is gnarly terroir, but all are battened

blithe to mattresses. Even the olden among them,
        catheters pebbled choke with sediment,
are in mangy comfort. The motherly solace of powder
        on bedchafe. Dreaming caffeine-free,

they don't want evicted from this quiet
        complete enough to hear yeast proofing
in kitchens, on genitals. They call foe
        the exam lamp of noon, the day on them

escapeless as credentialed hands, puckered latex,
        & the antibiotic pleas of a chaplain.
Natal light pranks the windowlip. The sun
        is a yellow-headed brat.

Otherlight

*What's between you & time
but a bail-bondsman?* Reads the flyer
tacked to the bulletin
at the Baptist Church. I'vent got anything

sage to say to that. But I know enough to know some would
claim elsewise. After pap passed on, &
when it was too smarmy outside even
for a top sheet, my grandmother slept

with whatever slack fabric she had
handy—an apron front, limp shift, or the hound
toothed hem of a housedress—covering her face
entire. She thought this wiling

would convince Death or any other
malevolence that might've come
to recoup her that she was already
ghosted. & having seen her in deep

caul, I'd agree
that she looked only gently
sinewed to this world. More than once
my cousin & I stood over her

during these naps she took to endure
the crude things
afternoon did to her body. *Let's play
like we're doctors: you smooth*

the sheet, I'll make the call. But locomotively
she drew breath, & I was too fixated
watching her gulp the same sunflower
embroidering off her apron over & over to see

to the postmortem. She sounded
like something that would make you regret
conducting a séance. The way she drooled
through the lean cloth, a murked-over window

into all that unlovely
personhood, simpled me. She had a candle
complexion. Her skin
was complicated as a Phoenician

sundown. But that pigment was brief. How peaceably
it grayed—oodles of bruiseflesh
dozing into bone. & in the final year, I could only dread her
patient taper. The viral

quietus. Now, decades later, level
eyed, I try & recollect some of her
shrewdery: *even if you can't outfox Death, you might
at least make him scratch*

his head for a spell. Or so I tell myself
was the gist of her
phantoming as I bear down on this empty page
that's like a white flag   I'm trying not to wave.

Bellyaching

Bless this queasy life oh lord
the palsy of a well-pump
you can't wash the slop off under
the chapped spigot. This outhouse
where I'm holed up
with the drizzling shits—
my stomach in enough knots
to earn a medal—the swollen room
of my rectum rented out
to these scum pipes
clogged with cess.
Drain-O that will leave you
longing for the dry
gushings to slacken
in the cemetery of your guts—
the small intestine a tombstone
with the liquor's sob-story scrawled in fat
on the droopy liver. The gallbladder
a potter's field where the greening bile
officiates in conditions of constant
flux. Rigor Mortis in the urethra
my piss shy as a monthling I do
simple addition & lickspittle sums
to coax it out like the creek
after a flood dragonflies & dung beetles
witness the mark no more
than a knife's girth that a moth
makes hush on my lips shut
my mouth like gauze spooled taut like a butterfly
bandage. There's this tow truck hauling hard
freight down the jammed highway
of my hind end double time I'm doubled up
& over again skull between knees
like I'm molting like I might stiffen
into the Sabbath the seventh day

of this godawful virus. Through woodpecker
chinks in the wall the moon pranks me
with its spotlight on these splinters
like little mealworms rooting in the white spackle
of my thighs. Beneath all this squelch
a leach-bed teething on subsoil
so rich it's gouted. What to blame
for this bloodletting this hot soda
fizzling out of my ass? Must have been
the cured meat we dolled up for supper
with all the trimmings
a week lapsed. The grease
on our lips like a whole bout
of leftovers. With single-ply
pages from the Sears & Roebuck catalogue
daubed like shrapnel in my rear
I waddle outside. My father
& I meet in opposite directions
on the homeward path
worried to an interstate
of packed dirt. We pass without words
just hands steepled in prayer
on our paunches
pregnant with regret.

Aesthete

My grandfather knew horses. In just a rind
of moonlight he could itemize them: withers, stifle, the fetlocks

fey & lyric. With his loose time, he bred savants
for dressage. There's just no other word

for the things they could do
ahoof. The image I have of back then is him

out in the smithereens
of a muggy season, drilling them. He'd take old plowhorses, oblivious

to anything but a coarse plod, & demented roans & manner them
until they could stop & turn

to statuary. Endure half
an hour in strict contraposto—the mouth

a stately wound, hamstrings taut enough to chord
in a somber key. I never understood that savage

acumen, or his fealty to the careworn
equus. Every evening, he'd rehearse them until absolute

dark & thereafter. Then he'd be up again at four a.m. to abuse
his eardrums digging

mineral for the National Mine Company. Come home dressed
in soot, the marginalia of three days

without sleep cluttering his eyes, & start anew. Saturdays, he fussed
with them for hours before a show, his tackwork

paternal & exact. & then in squinting awe I'd watch him, this man
who untangled his own hernia

with a box-cutter, become elegant. A poem
asaddle, he'd maestro his horse through its byzantine

paces, bringing up dust
in dainty *tsks*. The heat would have my t-shirt

clammed against me
like a membrane. & yet along he'd go at a peppery canter, sveltely

gotup in coat-&-tails. Not a bead
of angst on him anywhere. Hell, even his cowlick

laid docile. & when he'd win, the bargain
honorifics didn't do squat for him. The trophies were given away

to mildew & tarnish. & he didn't even spend
the prize money—the checks just became

pulp for his chickenhouse. To others in our bunch, it was queer
that this man who operated heavy

equipment for a living, whose fingers always smacked
of diesel fuel, would agonize over the stitch count

of a halter. Would look through a jeweler's loupe to make certain
that the braid his mare wore was squarely

in the Rhineland fashion. But to me it was nothing
short of bewitchment, watching him govern a ring. To hear him

give dictums in able French, his voice the octave of faraway
dynamite, & see the horse heed. To see anything on four legs

that rapt. It heartened me, knowing each pirouette & half-pass, each
delicacy was wrought by an animal he had swapped

a motorized garden tiller for—one whose blood was about as blue
as a foreclosure sign. That he could take something haggard, homely

stock, & learn it to move so neat of hoof, to gait & rein
sphinxlike over any pattern. Even back then, that buoyed. Let me fret

a little less about the dartboard
puberty had made of my face. But it wasn't until much later, after

I had a car payment & ulcer of my own, that I realized what he got
from it. What kept him out in the pasture, making geniuses. The sole

thing in his life that didn't just boil down to sweat
equity.

Pilgrim

My mother would've made a dandy pilgrim: she's pious
as hell & she doesn't just pretend
to like stale bread. She won't touch the stuff

unless it's spent a parched fortnight
in the toaster. Hardtack would've been white
truffle to her. Still, as we live & breathe & sin, she goes about the fine

aging of a sixty-cents-off loaf, de facto
sawdust, with an air
trafficker's rigor. She can't stomach error

even by the hairbreadth. But, in dealings with people, I've never
known her to be a taskmaster. & with family she's been Job's
breastfed sister. Even though dish-detergent kept her knuckles

grim as lug nuts, & calming the checkbook each month worried
stigmata into her pencil-finger, she was always the first to rummage
around for a kind word, a call

if you need me. & that empathy
was militant—I saw it in the maniac alms she gave, half
a paycheck, to the man she caught disemboweling

her childhood home. Together they wept & he rewired
all that copper himself. I saw it in the black snake
she set free from the glue trap in our laundry room

even though it hadn't rained for three months at least
& the whole holler was dying
to drape it over a fencepost

in folk penance. But she had no patience for shibboleths. None
for whiners, either. Me chief among them: all the times I wanted
to bitch about our sole toilet that didn't flush right, that any solid

waste made aspirate. Or about the dryer
that ran hot enough to cauter a slit-wrist & would tremor free
from its plumbing & trail you

zombified down the hallway—she'd tell me in plain
scald that three quarters of the world would war
over a finicky toilet, an awry dryer. That I was sitting

pretty. But, eavesdropping, I'd hear her choke
on that catechism as the Sclerosis made it less & less dreamable
to walk without a cane. To tend a meal, stand for a hymn. To storm

off after a spat. To be anything but rote, dependent. In the prayer
logs she began to keep, I'd wager there was a doubling
down: *fleshly life, haleness, knees*

that don't give backward at their crux
like a bowstring: these are mere bauble—fly me
from all that. & though, to this day & hour, she's never forgotten

herself, never done anything but bristle
tomcatlike from pity, I know she's been thinned. I see it
in the bicycle she pined to ride again parked forever

in cuckleberry vines, wisteria
for a front wheel. I see it on Sundays when she can't
genuflect, her face quarried from woe, during the invitation. Times

like these, reeling myself, I'm prone to imagine my mother's first
trip to this ink-goiter on the fracking map. Though Ohio
born, that summer she was cordial to the dumb

pant of East Kentucky; went through the dogbite
of July with tropic aplomb. Jolting along primly in a Lumina
with no hubcaps, she began to care for this place, its collective

mullet. Haired-over, untucked, rode hard & put up wet, she solaced
them all—thirty years & counting in the classroom. So many
owe her. But I'd say they're scot-free. She's not one to miser

favors. She even told me once: *for me, it's just never been politic
to let another know my heart.* & I'm selfsame. But, just
now, hearing her thresh

for sleep, I want
only to take her hand & hold it
through the friendless dark.

Local Delicacy

It's the waning night of the county fair & men have lined up

  to vomit off a swingbridge. The only light

is lampkept. Federated along one

  groggy keel, they void the Flash-Fried Oreo & butternut

schnapps from their middles

  with a Balkan violence, tennis shoes gone

cloven from too hard a gird. The wind catches

  & couriers their spew along like a beauty

pageant banner coming unknotted two rain-slewed

  stalls away. Passersby, straggling through the undoing

of pea-shooter booths & gawk tents—the dinged stakes, concertina

  wire, & patchwork laid out like scrap

vasculature—have to duck

  to miss the flock

of sick going just overhead. That smell

  is what the old hold-forths on the courthouse steps—their hearts

wardrobed in wist & triglyceride, each voice a husky

  pistolnote—with no small fondness call

    idjit stew.

After Breakfast, Knott County, 2007

Some places, the lawns are kept kempt. Year round
they're neat as pool table velvet. Some neighborhoods
have HOA & ADT signs stobbed in each yard
like heraldry. But I don't think you can get there

from here, where I'm loafing on the porch
of a house chewed
to osteoporosis by termites. All around me, there are weeds
swarthy with autumn. Cumulus

comes from the nostrils
of a snorting horse. My father
is asleep in his recliner, fossilized
milkfat on his lips. & I'm just waiting for the rest of the day

to tucker out, for the dark to come in like a young tough
past curfew, so I can again pull the smoldering
behinds off of lightning bugs & relish dad's
matte breath as he smokes & bleats

about how sorry I am. But for now, I just piss
acrid on an anthill, shoot marbles
with a slingshot through the dereliction
of a one-room schoolhouse, & mash a flashlight

against the crepe
paper eyes of a blind mule. I try to give him
secondsight. Midafternoon, my mother finally cracks
open the kitchen window & heaves

out the last bits of giblet & biscuit. The old smellhounds
loitering below squabble over it like heirs
to a gentle estate. My ugly god:
there's just nowhere safe to bury all that

time
I
killed.

Hormonal

Evening tampers with me. I dread it
    the way a moonshiner does
        Sunday morning. At supper, the jaw works

classically, but my insides are all
    amoil. Without restraint, I get to thinking on the wild
        oralness of chewing food. & then I've gone

& made a damn heathen
    revelry of mealtime. I look at my chair & am mindful
        of desks in the schoolhouse & the girls

that saddle them. There is altogether too much
    of them & it surpluses
        out the back & sides, white

profit. They seriously sit
    those desks. The ribbing on my steak knife
        distresses the heirloom

tableware. Things have vigor: the neonatal
    tenderness of this veal chop. The baby fat. I fork it
        till it coos. By six o'clock

news, I've pulled myself
    peach-fuzzless—the little weevils
        of hair against my papery chest

like an asterisk. Tonight's pathos piece: 16
    year old ties state's largest cherry stem
        with her tongue. The judges keep applauding

the integrity
    of her knot, its lithe classicism. Something *blue*
        collar & sensuous. I go out on the porch, starch

myself in the sneering air. The moon shows
      its side-boob. I take crisp breaths
            but, like a scope, my eyes tactify

onto the main road where a doe,
      desperate, drags her sex across blacktop
            in wormy rut. I hold myself

but not together.

Parts & Labor

Frenchman Mullins had a little
   hair-cutting place. Summers,

I'd make an odd dollar there
      sweeping up. Near to closing, he'd sauce

his utensils in Barbicide & flop down
   in the swivel chair to count

his moldy money, read each bill
      front to back like an old love

letter. The radio was stuck
   between stations, always

mewling. I'd fiddle
      with the dial while Frenchman

tallied his keep & squeezed
   the sebum from his nostrils

all absentminded. Afterward, satisfied
      or not with the turnout, he'd collect

the shambles of himself
   & go home

to his dented can of soup—widower's
      special. I'd stay behind

& tidy up: soap the linoleum, hand
   launder the day's linen—bibs, towels, aprons

the odor of iron. Lastly, I'd sweep the clippings
      into a feed sack & lug it

the better part of a mile
        to the sty, dump bits

of twenty different people
                into the trough

like someone paying tribute
        & watch the pigs, at first shy

as stakeout cars, start to flesh out
              the fog. The workmanlike sound

of their grazing, chewing
        sheer calcium. I remember

thinking they should've been
            salaried, laughing

at their idiot grins, teeth
        yellow as a business listing

                in the tri-county phone book.

Pure Fool

We had ham & Brie on
our saltines, fortified wine. & even though we were ill
met by the needling rain & springtime's
anarchic phlegm, it was a grand picnic. The way you saw things
whetted the way I saw things, so we gnawed on the hock
of conversation for hours. & never did it border on fatal

quaintness. The sky going
gunmetal, I recited some
choppy De Sade. Big oratorical haymakers. I thought I'd carpet
bombed your sense of certainty, decency. I thought I was telling
brimstone truths—putting the unlubed hydraulics
of your mind through their paces—but you were all

blasé in the face, & a great shudder of wind
went out of my sails. Then, seeing just how
wintry I was, coquettish you winked & let me ride
roughshod over your lips. Your breath
whorling with lunchmeat & curdled

hormone, we kissed. All schmaltz. Sidelong
the dusk went, day in its closing
scrimmage with night. My hands
moseyed up & down you stoic
as digestion. Layer after layer shucked, but I never struck
your weedy ulterior. So swank, you made me want to spell

my name with an umlaut; to till your garden
in something hipper than bib overalls. To undo a watermelon
ascot instead of these lusterless galluses. We shared a few minutes
where months happened. & by the time I sobered up, it was noir
dark, & the cool was nipping
hoarse at our voices. So we repaired to the pew

seat in my Chevy Celebrity. Again I wanted
to say something climactic to you. Something
axiom-shattering. But there was this heady & blanketing
squeamishness from the aftermarket exhaust
tiptoeing through the cab, so my quips weren't nearly
hardboiled enough. In the end, I just ceded quiet. Didn't feel

any less a man for the tabula rasa
look on my face when again & again you dynamized me
from crotch to cowlick.

Rite

after Arnold van Gennep

My hamstringer: I've never done anything
without watching myself do it. So the first time I drank

to unanimous drunkenness, it was like getting my walking papers
from a 30-ought-6. Somebody'd pawned me

Hermes' sneakers. I was winged chic. Or what a peddler of showponies
        might term deft of shoe. We, me & Delbarton
& Goodnight, were drinking gin through a straw

out of shag carpet—quaffing in with such vim it was apt to tornado
a rib, mug corpuscles—until it felt like a phrenologist, starved

for ethos, had me calipered by the sinuses. This was our usual:
        scrounging more lint & cat litter than buzz. But that night
was alien to the others. Delbarton's pap

was the eight days a week kind of drunk, bad to racket & rambunct.
He drew SSI, but one Tuesday a month he was a scab

driver for the rock quarry, hauling shale along the matchstick tendons
of creeks & hollows, ratfinking wages for the hourlies. He'd be in bed

with a bottle sludged full of meanness the evening before, so as to take
a molasses-paced relish in drinking the light away, but still wake up

with minimal eulogy. But, that night, he must've gotten himself
malign with the wife, who drove him to the living room floor

with a 3-wood. &, mid-crumple, this fifth of Beefeater fluttered
        from his hands like a graveside dove.
You can augur the rest. Goodnight said *Lord God this gin*

tastes like airport cologne. Woah there, Fauntleroy,
    you'nt been to no airport. My tongue was already lawless,
& things beyond fathom were taking form at the municipal limits

of my eyes. Every sup was a guffawing peal of thunder,
    & the backwash fizzed genial against my tonsils.
But soon we were gin-poor, & my mind went elsewhere: yowling

into the nonsense end of a straight pipe, sniffing what stirred.
    There was this griping
in my gut, but I wanted more likker like you want something

womansmelling in bed next you. It felt like I was all over
    creation, but I hadn't graduated from the wingback,
still just sitting there in the significant

grooves my ass had begat. So while they were in the kitchen
    vulturing around a freezer full of good aim, I doused
out the old man's Rapture stash. It was a pint of vodka—spuds

rotgut enough to harelip a Tsar—bobbing in the flushbox. Through it
I wolfed. & they found me scowl to scowl with the unchaste

veneer of the commode, all my assets
liquidated. Windless in those doldrums, it was rocket science to keep

my keel even. But the moment I felt their hot concern on my stubble,
    I was sabers out like J.E.B. Stuart at Brandy Station,
like the Black Prince laureled in slaughter at Poitiers.

Why you got to be so choleric? Goodnight said. He chided me
in the face & my sight was severaled. Between the ears, there was lupine

static. In defeat, I was Roland dutifully eating
    Saracen arrows. I figured I'd just laze a minute,
take stock, but wouldn't you know

they already had me quicklimed, totalized in salt. I was
        aslosh on the cooling board
of their joined hands, forearms latticed slipshod, & the procession

back to the futon was afflicted. Mussed by drink, they brained me
        against anything with an edge. But I wasn't cross about it.
& that noise wasn't my head

dribbling against ground, a bindle of trauma.
        That's just what it sounds like
when you hit paydirt.

If I Know Me

I am chromed over. June & its rabid
maximums keep stirring me into this porridge

of bedlinen. You have to be half a yogi
to get unclung. But squelching to the toilet, waiting

for the pap on my chest to go luxuriously
tepid, I see the shadow of my father

like caulk along the kitchen wall. He is staring into the harvest
tinge of the fridge light, the Freon trilling

kindly across his face. What to make
of this lategoer? Every wretched thing, even the air

conditioner, is conked out. But here he is sleuthing
through the condiments, a jar of pickled trotters

already waylaid on the counter. I can hear the hour
old cud mortared flavorless in his cheek. But still he's eking

the last splats of liverwurst from its loaf. & gingerly he stretches
both arms into the fridge's

chapped nether, comes out with a quart of eggnog. All that Yuletide
has aged crudely, turned

calico with pus. Yet, swilling it, his gizzard goes up & down
hectic as a dumbwaiter. After, he gives his brunt

to a lean black stool, & for a time just sits there
with this Quaalude smirk. I say his name over & again but he doesn't

twitch a mite. Doesn't do a thing but lag there, looking
like cut-rate taxidermy. Though it's not long before he begins

to retch—bout after spiteful bout, the sick caking
Rorschach on his nightshirt. Antiquely stooped, mossed

in upchuck, he is knotty
as a grubbed stump. Again I speak at him—crickets.

Only when I lay on
rousting hands does it click: he's been embalmed

in sleep this whole time. The blank in his eyes
says low bandwidth. But shockingly

sniper-esque: he eases his elbows
onto the linoleum islandtop, parks his chin there

all Irish Setter, & answers me
with a snore. & it's in this shaggy moment—watching

his impoverished sleep, whiffing those hiccups so
umami with botulism—that I piece together why

I've never been able to get enough
of too much.

Nightwatchmen

wipe their asses
                                        with the ads

in titty magazines. They're reminded
                                        of what their good for

nothing fathers gave them
                                        when the fine print

reads a hemorrhoid. Up off
                                        the porta-john, they look down

at the jambalaya that's left
                                        for flies. The night

is a slow-cooker. They return
                                        to their black post

& tasks that are seldom
                                        more than irksome. Almost bovine,

mining equipment grazes
                                        the strip-job fog.

By the foreman's trailer
                                        on dual sawhorses

plans were laid
                                        to level something. Come morning,

once their shift
                                        has lapsed, they'll ghost out

onto the county road
                                        half addled

& wrap their cars around

                              power poles

like a wedding ring.

Crowfare

Some only know them by their crew
cut feathering, plumage
kept to a martial taper. Or how clinically
they chart the human
ruckus, those prodigies
of decomposition. But so unlike
the buzzard, though, who gorges

mongrel on any old haunch
of carrion—a plebe for rot—the crow
dines with propriety, pecks
the forage off its bill
on a littered tampon. The talon always
so fussily tidied
afterward in a bird

bath—the owl, that well
studied miserabilist, watching on
judicially. My father once guaranteed to me
that a crow knows
the GDP of the neighborhood
it circles. *They certainly don't
patrol the holler,* he said.

*Now your mother's neck
of the woods, Northern Ohio of the industrial
strength carcinogen, funereal quiche, & gore
capitalist, that's a crow
kind of outfit. We've only got buzzards
& no-gumption vultures. Don't even mention
a raven. Anymore, they're only in stuffy
old Europe & stories*

*written by candlelight. They beg
the monocled. A Dukedom comes*

*with its very own gross
of ravens nowadays. Like a sinecure,*
I say, & toe over the turpentine. *Well shit.*
We are housepainting in a subdivision
three hours from home. Above us, crows

read the newspaper
with their noses—getting up to speed
on breakfast: something shot
less than sportingly in the yard
next us. I watch my father
watch their skyful of dark
reveille & imagine he must think *O*

*to be propertied, solvent, to be enough
of a bona fide that a crow might drink
the pupil rheum from a thing I have
enough dominion over to decide when
it should die.* & to be spared even
their shipshape digestion. Again, unlike the lifetime
of buzzards he's seen halfwittedly

chawing the easymeat
from roadside spoilage, then chucking
up the surplus founder. He wants
to unwitness the slack
dewlap. Tea had,
the crows will browse the high literature
of limb & shingle & power

line—tar-paper cosmopolitans—until their dinner
cedes to the quick hospice
of a drainage culvert or spice
garden. & beneath them I'll continue
avoiding my father's
toilsome eye, the ultramarine
sore as a gash. But the white

paint on his wrist
is on mine too. We are
togethered. It's tribal, this paint
undiluted by rustwater, iodine, or
miscellaneous whatnot. & in the fungal silence
of the truck, plugging home hours later, we are still
ligatured—my father, ornery in his hunger
to have, & me woebegone with this cold

savvy: being moneyed is like being in love
or heaven, you never get out
what you put into it.

Love in the Time of Company Towns

Nothing worth nothing ever happens
after midnight. Coroners & dairy

farmers alike have told me this, & you should believe
every atom of it. But, then again, a godgiven rule

is humbled by its exception. Tonight, for instance, I am
inevitable. You & me, your curls tasseling out

like a 4-H project, are hoofing pell-mell
down the mountainside to the birthing hips

of the Big Sandy, hallooing *there is no such joy
in the pharmacy as on the road thereto.* Boneheads

to the letter of the law. Eyes amok with dilation, I want the deed
to the way this swimming hole looks just now—all bluing

& moonburnt. Vague twang of chum. The cattail
astir like tooth-torn garters. Usually, I'm too gummed up

in everydayness to appreciate this
claptrap idyll. But right this second I need no convincing

that both my feet are planted angelic in the heartland
of the real. With ring fingers you fishhook

my nose. *Get a royal whiff of that,* you say, & I mainline
the menstrual zest of a river in July. Lo-Fi

sublime. Water busks over the bosom of stones. Lusty
crickets won't take maybe for an answer. Tomorrow surely

there'll be another frog-strangling rain. Too spongey to ply
a trade, earn a troglodyte living, roofers & loggers might

mass here to fish, drink, lie, swap
lore. Might connive against their foremen, some

litigious homeowner. & I too will be out
another day's greenback roughage. But this doesn't peeve—

I can always binge
you through the billable hours. *Thwack*. I just went to palm

one of your glands petite, but the drowsy piles of rock
we were idling against made a tattletale sound & with malice

came apart. We are side-by-side on the grass now, sides
splitting. *Chalk a line around us as we lay, & this'd be right*

tragic. More star-crossed than Heloise & Abelard. Still airy
& elfin from the vertigo, you ask if those are the names

of the teacher & student who got caught holding pagan
angles in the supply closet at the vocational school? *More*

or less, I say, & course my hand up your spine
like a Geiger counter—pausing above the pastoral

inflections, the haute scoliosis, to *bleep* animatronic. Grinning,
our fingers duet. We are close enough to know each other

biblically. So close I can hear the rods
clank in your back when you move

your mouth to mine. Now we are not talking
swine futures or the Technicolor horrors that haunt

the CSPAN ticker. There is noise, but not a trifle of that. What home
steads between us: sighs, yips, small gallantries, air

sacs daubed in ancestral gunk. Right now, there's strictly this
strep throat patter—hot, thoughtless. Like a gamboling lamb, you go

to & fro. The flats of my feet sizzle
with hookworm.

Visiting the Barn the Night Before I Burn it Down

In the stall, I admire the white bloom
of horse bones

                                    sprouting through the carpet
                                    of straw & moldered shit, piss

stewed dirt. Briskets
thrifted clean by crows. Nothing

                                    here now but the raw nerves
                                    of a housecat skulking leanly

through haycoffin dark, pouncing
on the year-old

                                    shadow of a rat. Cairns
                                    of cobwebbed tack in the loft:

halters, curry combs, silver teeth
broken off the corroded spoke

                                    of a spur. Souvenirs
                                    from when I was young & yet

unfucked: yearbooks rewritten
by floodwater, baby clothes

                                    hemmed to fit
                                    termites & earwigs, empty bottles

of Bute that made my tired pony
step high. A nail in the wall

                                    I hammered all to hell & left
                                    with a crooked thumb—the blood

belched out like water
from a bad tap. Bats flap through

                        their old motions in the crawlspace
                        of my chest. Outside, a possum

practices its death & even tricks
the ticks off its back. The moon

                        is a cleaned plate. I call this place
                        what it's become: kindling.

II

"In a rich man's house, there is no place to spit but his face."
—Diogenes the Cynic

"All your sorrows have been wasted on you if you have not yet learned how to be wretched."
—Seneca

Zeitgeist & Gristle

Always & above all: dread dishonor. Too many men
mealy-mouth through life, teetering
foddershocks. They're agreeable as memory
foam. Hug up awedrunk against any fool
with unimpeachable posture. I would know—I subsist
in a city. Frazzling out in all directions: uncombed

concrete. At soft dark the car alarms cluck
hen-skittish, & everyone has their own boutique
neuroses. Shit, most people here are in mad love
with their own prattle. They misknow
the lowliest smudge on a spectacle lens
for profundity—the sun going

tweed behind clouds at twilight. The streets
are insufferable with their bathos
vendors, people hocking t-shirts
pimpled rhubarb so you can so bravely wear that trademark
hurt on your sleeve. But my world
wasn't always milquetoast. I came up

in a craggy mountain town the name
of Fractured Jaw. Most folks there had spines
smelted rebar from busting rock, tending Hell's back
acre. O the almighty cartilage. & how I miss the grizzled
democracy of winter: everything looked like a ditchline.
Nothing to capture your sight, just manholes

burping medieval & the wind bank-vault-stiff. A cold
so encompassing your blood came out pleasant
as sorbet. & dearly I miss the cemeteries cause the graveslabs
brooked no gossip. It was a dry county, but the WET
sign crackling chemo-green outside the bootlegger's shack
was the zodiac of all want. Yes, you kept

your woes confidential. Counted as accolade each day
the lord saw fit to let you trudge on
unsmitten. & best of all, you never had to deal with the sidewalks
full of malnourished loons, each blubbering *help me, my pre-frontal
cortex is on the fritz*. Thugs demanding CBT at pocketknifepoint. I itch
for home, but just couldn't hack it there. I suffered

meltdowns, prissy melancholia. & the doctor would only prescribe
push-ups, aggressive doses
of contact sport. Finally, the High Sheriff escorted me
to the county line, sent me on my kooky way with a bone
pulping handshake & this slim treatise
on emotional continence by Epictetus. Now I'm no better

than Al Capone: bass fishing in his swimming pool, syphilitic
to the gills. Scratch that; I'm a long way worse. At the very least
he wasn't pussified. Wasn't sapien pudding. So I guess there's nothing
left for me but group therapy—wincing at the quiver of every necktied
wattle—& jotting down these poems where I ache
for Fractured Jaw. Feebly, for ballast, I repeat

our town motto: *No
Zeitgeist, All Gristle.*

Sleep Apnea

There is always something to be said
for regularhood: the familiar

    falter of a barstool, the cold fidget
    that creaks a tree stand, pipe fitting, pissing

        mineral, breathing asbestos, paying up
        union dues. The kind of doggedness

that translates to devotion. To this end
I am mouthing

    my blessings into a trundle mattress
    beside a snoring woman that knows me

        better than I'd like to be known. The window
        wears no drape. The moon is a fistful

of ripe light. The way
the sheet pleats

    below her thighs is somehow French
    as the names of those poets I love

        to mispronounce. But I can't stop
        thinking of another woman—

the one in that painting
on the label of those pint bottles. If this were a cock

    rock ditty I'd call her the Queen
    of all I've seen—that coal-eyed so & so.

        But this is uncut
        memory & I'm just trying to let it be

bygone. Hours ago, the woman sharing this mattress
asked me what do you dream? I said

>   I dream as always
>   of my own death. How I want my wake

>> to be remembered
>> as the gray matter

between effigy & pyre. How I picture a young man
in the graveyard reading by matchlight

>   my name. This cracks her
>   up. She knows the joke

>> is that I'm hideously sincere. Dying young
>> doesn't mean you live forever she said

& like a wheel in deep mud sputtered
to a stop, slept. I'm grateful she took me

>   for forthright, cause I'm not fit to give her
>   the blood-candid truth: I dream of watching

>> my grandfather stagger home
>> through the wooly snow, my breath

backfiring on the window glass. He is pulling
from a quart jug. He steps across the ice

>   with such discretion it's as if he fears waking
>   even his own self. But of course he slips

>> & sunders the jug. I see him hit his knees
>> like someone begging a favor

& lap up every star
mirrored in the spill.

       I can't take all that
       & turn anywhere

              but inward. It's just too much
              to inherit.

Say Wise Things or Die, Egghead

Peachy to meet you, but my thoughts
are thistling. I might need a New

York Minute to trim them. Luckily, I just had
a cigarette. Unluckily, it was the nausea cig. Every pack

has a nausea cig & a euphoria cig. Someone nigh
always bums my euphoria cig. Queasy

as she goes, I guess. Anywho, we best be getting gone: Stop
Drop & Roll donut work in hell. True

love ain't nothing but easygoing
heart disease. A common denominator between wooing

& winterizing homes: the rustier
the roof, the wetter the basement. Yes, I'm talking

womankind: sign, tangent, & secant
of all our affections!! But there's troves more

to me than redhead apologetics. That there is just a throwaway
filet of scholarship. *Timely, timely* the critics crumpling up

eviction notices in my hippocampus say. But, at core, I know my prose
needs policed. It's dastard smut. A liverspot

limo to the spanking new vomitoriums
in Torment. We Pharisees: we're overbrained

& underworked. Our excuses are so poor they qualify
for TANF in the reddest state (don't get it twisted—you won't find me

grousing about a safety net, but it shouldn't rest easy
as a blankety-blank hammock). & the limp

morals—trust me, Balaam's ass sets up
buxom in a wonk's mind. Without, within

we're weapons-grade sinful. We take knees
to sharecropping & Southron history. Heatstroke was just

the scent of the season. Many-throated, the fates say
somewhere along the way you started to think you weren't

part of the food chain anymore. You can't sugar
over biology, primate. Start peopling. Yet here I sit, sipping

the sedate grog of philosophy, mulling over
my unseaworthiness. The old legislation was just quill pens

& curlicues & spliced commas. What does it say to a clay
eater? All he understands is gout & government cheese, a stiff whiff

of grapeshot. Can't you smell
those skunky chromosomes from here? Sheesh. Machine-gunning

gibberish, am I? No, smart mouth, I'm just begging
America to stop digging her own cussed grave

with a fork & knife. Right now it'd take the jaws
of life to span that sea

to shining sea waistline. Translation: those britches are so tight
I can see your religion. Uh-oh—so this is where the mood goes

somber, bibleblack? It's getting right
smothersome in here. & you look like you're up for a promotion

at the headache factory. No need to mope; there's no bull
from them papists that says you have to stop living

deliciously. Just cool it with the foie gras. Goosegrease
is kingly steep. Now you don't seem like the sort to henpeck

an anecdote, so I won't tar & feather you
with too many facts. Just one more hairy truth: binge eaters

& Commissars both know what bliss it is to pig out
on somebody else's ruble. Apologies, but my own way

is all I can afford to pay. So here's where we part, man
in the pantyhose mask. But take heart: I was born with nothing

&, knuckles white as driven snow, I've managed to hang on
to most of it. Best of luck

pistol whipping the next schmuck.

Pitching Fits

Manhood: no one coaches you through
how uncouth it can be. A glorified coop
with no furniture, my rent-controlled abode. Just this tintype
of smut on the wall where

the couch used to sit. Before the Big
Lots repossessed it. Some chicken
scratch whittled on the floor that for all I know says *Nebuchadnezzar
Wuz Here*. Beside it, a warped LP: *Whipping Post—The Extended

Rendition*. Enough pubes to make a chia pet. Dr. Pop, absinthe
& a week old meatloaf sandwich, sans catsup. I've got a lot

of things to learn. This is the skinny: I frequently mess up
& mix darks with whites, cut the crud

that liquor leaves behind with beer
flat as my uncle swears the earth is (don't fret, for hygiene I swish
my mouth sterling with Sprite). Each day is a cockfight
between my laziness—my roadkill verve—& my ambition

to tell it like it ought to be. To tell it
ornery. *Don't talk too colorful; it hurts
my old purpling heart,* Mom says. *Son, take a gander
at your hands. What have they built?* Dad says

& wags his sandy head. He's Melungeon so his tan
never blanches. 65 & his skin is still

beachfront property. But I'm wan as scurvy. All the paler
for sleeping each day away, hoot-owling through the night. *Thank God

the game warden's gone
blind* is the first line of this koan I'm writing. It'll be
the lodestone of my manuscript, *The New
Brutalism*. It'd be on shelves already to thundering acclaim if only

some philanthropic soul would spot me
the postage. *That boy's brain is a dreamsicle
in the July swelter*—so say the employable men in my clan, the ore
barons & thoroughbred janitors alike—*he'll never get the knack*

*of nothing substantive. I don't even think we could make
a TIG welder out of him.* & they're not fibbing. I flipped

through a magazine about the Marne at Wal-Mart
& gave myself trenchfoot. You better believe

Medicaid doesn't cover that. *Honey, you sure are a hemorrhoid
on the be-hind of the taxpayer.* That's what the nurse
practitioner told me in her sunny lilt. Verbatim. I'm supposed to
spend tomorrow helping myself

to some catalytic convertors with a jailbird cousin, but damn
if that don't sound ponderous as leading
the Israelites clear out of the wilderness. So indubitably it's back
to beanie-weenies & spitballing this

homely verse. Pencil cocked, I put on a pipefitter's hat & pretend
I'm working a big job, time

& a half pay.

Sons of Perdition, KY

The dog was long dead, but its eyes still looked
        owlish at me. Puddled there

in cartoon red, beetles spelunked across it, the color
        & character of tobacco drool. Midwinter, I was thicketed

in severe material, hardly able to articulate
        my arms & legs. But Toy had stripped down

to bare suet, trying to haggle it
        alive. Swivelnecked, face flushed carbide, he made urgent

sounds at me. It didn't matter. Words could be spoken
        loud as you pleased but the wind

was a felon, pocketed them. I went & hunkered over him. Effort
        & wispy genetics had tonsured his hair. Only three past

the hour of thin meridian, & already the light
        was pigeoning away. A chloroformed scene. Above, buzzards

saddled the day's last vividry, the clouds
        novicely crocheted. Toy's head

was sumped down in his collar
        turtlewise. *Whoever owns up to this*

is galactically fucked. His voice was like rustling
        through tissue paper. I could see February

sharding all over him, his shoulders
        funnel-caked. Another bluster & his crouch gave out

& he was on his ass in the snow & froth, severed
        umbilicus.

. . .

I know it was one of those lard-asses from up Hemp Patch, Toy
said. *They're still sore about them chickenfights.* He was overtop
the firepit. In it he flinted a wagging bouquet of flame.

They did it sure. He rose, yawned boomingly. *I'm pure
tired.* The night was cornmeal-bright—the air so edged
& blatant it felt star-whetted. Hillsides ablotch with winter. *I wish*

I was drunker than a warlord, Toy said. I imagined him that
next day—underemployed, feudally minded—ribbiting
mufflerless into the chokehold of this holler, then another. Asking

the incontinent & ankle-braceleted *Who
made a pancake outta my dog?* Getting back a faceful of moldy
dunnos, the shrill guillotine of screen doors. Fall had been a page

out of the almanac—vines & stalks so expectant the harvest
had to be C-sectioned off them. A beef or so was tattooed
to death by lightning, but all

in all a bumper yield. Fieldwork was regular. Now what
was he to do: go guileless
into the sphincter of a mountain & bully ore? Live

like a varmint on the corn
dole? I didn't begrudge him his miniature
narcissisms, a martyred dog. Of course he spied

conspiracy everywhichway, thirsted to get the narrative
by its nape & thump free some sense. So in wooden competence
I passed that night, month, decade nodding along with him. Why

keep tab? I knew that next day the sun would still trek
the sky at its dauntless putter, a sclerotic man
on his Rascal scooter. I knew the firmament

would still wad up ashen
as an old pact at 4pm. Me & Toy, what use did we have
for calendered time?

Crowbarring into a Schoolhouse at an Obscene Hour

Trouble makes us
hunt out the places where we knew
fatter times. That's gospel, but still
my hackles are up. Sitting here in the same migraine
beige desk I did as a thirteen-year-old, I can't
outmuscle the feeling that I'm about

to be born. Sentimentality: when you give
more tenderness to a thing
than its creator. It's told that God's love is broad
shouldered enough to bear even the louses
that sublet the comb-over on a child
diddler, but I can't figure why he'd give

two hoots about how phantasmic the fish
patties tasted at my grade school. I swear, reminiscing
concusses you. Right now, I know I'm credulous
as a dental patient: even the exposed
bulb in the nurse's office, gray as a hundred
cases of flu, looks transcendent. & the monoxide

vroom of an old hand dryer wafts across the ear
as mere purr. But I can't relish any of this like
I'd like: in 5-7 business days, they're intent
on dozing this building down
to stud & ion. & in the asbestos they'll lay
a victory garden, & AmeriCorps greenhorns will teach

crop eugenics to hungry people, hand out packets
of cantaloupe seed to pensioners. They humanely think
we're all Neanderthals. But forked light
from a sudden squall reassures me
that the young still carve their hellacious
lusts into the desktops. & through its trachea

tube the thunder tells me *don't*
dwell. In the hallway, my finger-ends rake across
the maimed lockers, & it kills me that I can't help
but halt at #39, the one with the hoax
bottom, where my good buddy
Clay-boy used to stash pouches

of Skoal Citrus. After recess I'd nab a few
whenever I wanted to
flutter my brain. & swooningly I take stock of #48, hoping
against hope that the note I left the first girl I ever held
hands with will still be crammed in there
somewhere. It said *let's run away*

to Tahiti. We'll live on love & papaya. Thrice now
I've been married, but recalling her I still
feel the earliest chigger bites
of longing on my lower half. That teases to mind
this oily joke I used to bandy back
& forth with Clay. It had to do with a man

named Enis. For the sake of it, I tell the joke
to no one. But my voice tripped out
peculiar, as if I'd simply
leased it. I was of a firm mind to call
Clay the other day, but wouldn't you
know his sister answered, & she said his tongue

had capsized in his mouth from the months
of chugging Robitussen. That his ex
ex-wife had left with the kids, feathered
a new nest with some local lawn mower
mogul, & that Clay was altogether low
as the blue jeans

on a bulimic. It's the bafflingest thing: we never know
we're living in a pat of butter
until it blinks.

Diatribe of the Runner-Up in a Piddling Local Election

If you happen upon a man from Letcher County, knock
him flat. He'll already know
the why, the wherefore. That place is rotten
with southpaws & anemics. & there even
the Christlike suffer from derangement
of the tear ducts—always snotting or wailing. To this
I'd swear an affidavit. But mercy is a virtue: I won't beat
a dead horse & bring up how tectonically

stupid they are. How all their gray
matter has been gnawed out
by Creutzfeldt-Jakob's. How grubby
backstrap from a 1 & 1/2 point yearling has left their gaze
slack & smarmy as anchovies in an apocalypse
proof tin. Upcountry dense

is an understatement. & it goes without saying that they all smell
like smoldering ozone. Abominable breath to boot. From snarfing
squirrel brains & eyeshadow crayon. Anything
to appease their Pica. & the weather: dismal
is too clement a word—stormfall daily
makes dulcimer music in the dingiest key. Weeds
overflush every fencerow, but there's no toolage
to chasten a bratty crop. & God forbid you're after any

municipal outreach, or aiming to foster
community: those folks will only donate blood
to a barroom floor. They wouldn't know
what a competent civil servant looked like
if one was to the knuckle in their prostate. Here's
my naked surmise: they'll be electing Vandals

& Visigoths over that way until the behemoth
engine block at the core of the earth
finally cracks. Doubtless it's a great comfort to a moron
to see other morons pulling strings, but that doesn't

acquit their idiot voting. They'll throw in
with any demagogue, any pork-barreler
who'll share a noxious supper with them & swear
to see about gentling those pill-peddler charges

the state has against their uncle
or mutant nephew. I'll work
like a borrowed mule for my constituents. But uprightness
is a strike against you in our times. Now it's seedy
panache that fills the gymnasiums. Enough dolor: I'm glad
to report that one county over, in the land

of Knott, it's all power & light. Cell phone service
is stalwart, & there's a monster
bass boat in every third yard. Better still, people don't rear
back from your *howdies* & *how goes its* like spitting
cobras. & here & now I'm witched
no more by rueful loomings. Even in the creaky
scruff of this bed where my great & lesser uncles did much
of their dying, my sleep

is mothball bliss. I wouldn't hoodwink you: they should bottle
this town & sell it as spiritual
colonic, cause the heretic germ is absent from this crowd. Just
yesterday I treated myself to a cherry snowcone at the First
Baptist fundraiser. It heartened
me to learn they called that flavor *God's*

Hemoglobin. So smack dab I decided to hang
on democracy's cross for these people. To stomach
the backbiters & peacocking parliamentarians for another
term in their stead. Here're the good
tidings: mine will be a name
on the ballot next fall because there never was
a nobler electorate. & crony, nothing would
tickle me more than adding your X
to my roster of esteemed backers. Scrawl

                        right here, please.

Every Day is Like Sunday

God always speaks to me
like hot grease
on a blouse. Sudden
enough to murmur

the heart. When I'm at the stove, worrying
over breakfast, & the whites of the eggs run
into something that resembles his Son's
fuming tunic. & later, when I'm up to my goof

bone in a sink
chatty with dishes, the soapcurds going in
tender disbelief over my hands
like Thomas. He's there in the family

room, in the ignorant
parboil of noon, the TV turned on
a local-access fishing show, when I'm folding
laundry. When I'm liable to nurture

a quiet, ladylike spite
for my two sons & husband—who has the horsepower
of a floor mop—sawing logs. He's there when I'm ruing
all the dewy choices

I made in girlhood. I don't know
where he'll be when I'm going through this whole
rigmarole again for the sake
of their lunch & supper. When bitterness settles in me

like buzzards in a treetop. & he'll be lost
to me still tomorrow morning, in the grocery
store parking lot when the car won't start, the sun
on me like acetylene, & it's two hours

till I can get a stranger to give a jump
that doesn't take. & after, when I go to the bank
& clean out our account & it's just enough
to pay the tow truck driver

& shiftless repairman, I like to think
he'll at least be there
to damn the moneychangers. I like to think it's him
making himself known

on my way home, when every pothole I hit
is shaped like a heart.

37.4029° N, 82.8063° W

On the two-lane there is a snake
pulled to black & cherry
taffy. It was a dually, leaving

skidmarks so deep they're Neolithic. In the gutterline, bloat
ballooning it, the aft-legs of a stray that very truck hit last week
articulate needlessly in the cretin breeze. We've got to vote

a new dogcatcher in. The incumbent's get up & go
has got up & went. He spends all his taxpaid
time in the silk-draft of the druggist's window unit, chewing

fat. The sky at dawn was nuclear. Forecast says a vagrant
rain might pass through. Maybe that will cologne the rancid
pith of salmonella. But doubtless the August sun will be back

for a last cutthroat westering. What is this brigandage? To wake
up each morning in the brown
glower of unwashed bedclothes, mites & knits

in diaspora across you. A stomachful of potted meat & Mad
Dog 20/20 like tangled fire. To waste all day shitting
saltpeter, studying the degeneracy

of the wainscoting. Here, if something ends, it ends
in attrition. There's an old wives' tale about cutting
your nose off to spite your face: there was this man, a smallholder

of backward means, who scrimped together a war ransom
for a cow that gave store-bought milk. It came out of the udder
pasteurized. He plumed himself on that heifer's yield. He'd trot it out

like a doorprize whenever he had company & make it give big
frothing samples. One night, drunk, he forgot to hasp its stall
completely shut, & the cow got loose. For three days, grief-skittered,

the farmer gnawed hangnails. Finally the cow moseyed home
prodigal, swatting gnats. The man necked it garishly, hands going
epileptic all over like buffing a car. He even went down low

to bask in the pecan
cloy of unrelieved teats. But, alas, the cow had been
into an onion patch, soured

itself. With a milk pail, he berserked it. That whole week, he
was in bed feverish, that smell still aroot in his nostrils, jarring
the cheek bones. He thought it was bereaving pangs, that it might

always persist. But one morning he woke to an unchoking—crisp
scents. It had all just been a bout
of foul sinuses. The cow hadn't impurity.

To most, this would just be cozy
nonsense: a sentiment some company could water
down to a five-word signboard dangling perfectly

nitwit in the kitchen of suburbanites who pay someone else to cook
palate-challenging meals for them. But to me & mine, it's about
right. That incisorless man lives up the way, & the cow

is in the drainage ditch—a festered blimp
beside the strays & snakes (he borrowed an end
loader to push it over). & I'm still on the toilet, counting failures

in the wainscoting. The mist speaks its dizzy piece
before the sun finally chars it away
in an after-rain tantrum. I'm drinking the very thing that keeps me

indentured to this commode. I'll probably still be here
in September, & by then even the trees will be hued
to hemorrhage.

Codependents

After a week of that
infidel living, there was barely enough
of you to drape a chair. I was home alone but miles
from lonely, reading a dime
Western about this marshal who's not afraid
to let what he keeps holstered

on his hip do the talking, when in you
typhooned. *My chakra is all out
of whack,* you said, & went completely
coral reef on the living room floor. You reeked
like a wine press—like the Mezzogiorno's

surliest grapes—& I could already envision your Accord
bogged someplace in the black
gumbo that tenacious rain makes
of a clay road. All of a sudden, the TV kept howling
zoinks. The cathode tubes were snagged

on the climax of an old *Scooby-Doo.* Shaggy just found out
who did it. What is it about you that can even
stutter a syndicated broadcast? What nasty
mesmerism? If desire is just a parlay
between tact & appetite, then you were the damned
armistice—you rode me

to treaty. Showed me poise
was just the diplomat's grift. & always you claimed your Alpha
was anarchy, indulgence your Omega, but those piss
ant words don't do it a lick of justice. Then as now
you nightmare me. & I can't even begin to give
that particular dervish its due. Only a few crumbs

of sleep before I woke to an angel
food cake in the oven the consistency
of a Merriam-Webster, every ounce of cookware
exotic with antibodies. The sun was a cold yolk
on the Works Cited that all your swatted
centipedes & roaches made of the breakfast nook. & you still

so rampant in the bathroom that I couldn't get any
barf in edgewise. & believe me when I tell you that
spew was rich as six rugged feet
up a bull's ass. So many weeks limped by
as such—you thatched in vice, swaying from bannister
to bookcase, demolishing things like imminent domain

in a maxi dress. Me slipping
into your blind spots, nibbling
tinfoil to purge the stress, blood
combustible as fracking runoff. Even your most benign
yammer could slingshot my pulse
through the synaptic rafters. Until some morning I'd find you

sober as a proctologist, toothbrushing the human
humus out of your delicates. That night, you'd usually beckon
me to bed at a respectable hour, straighten
my rudder. & for a month I'd let the memory of that one
jubilee simmer over like the dope
they give after gall stones. But there was no getting shed

of the fundamental taint. All those innings
we went together, & I never wised up. Never entertained
wising up. So, sure as the chicken
starved preacher lopes through the doxology, you'd welcome
back all your graceless habits. & I'd abide. Dangerously
loyal, I'd start patching up the fallout

shelter of myself—digging trenches, shoring battlements. But
the gird never matched the bang. Facing you, my city
always got sacked. My myrrh, my frankincense

delight: in spite
of ourselves, didn't we
have a galloping good time?

Injury to Insult

You threw coffee
in my face.
We feuded too long—
it had gotten cold.

The Hay Sufferer

He couldn't gather breath because of the army
surplus green bricked in his nose holes. *I know this
is unbecoming,* he said, *but the pollen
has me noosed.* Free he milked
a thin viper of slime. *I'll declare: congestion
can absolutely scatterbrain you. All my years*

*I've been a serf to bad sinuses. I fear it's made
an altogether glum man of me.* There were gangly black vultures
in his eyes when he said this. *Even in my salad days—
back when these old penny-loafers I'm wearing
wore a store-shine—you couldn't have convinced me
that my ears were anything more than a rumpus room*

*for yelllowjackets, what with the buzzing & carrying on. No
luck with women, neither. Even though I was head to heel
a sturdy character, & entrepreneurial as any H. Alger, always
my pluck failed me. & for all of it I indict
these devil sinuses. Every box social or barn festivity
was during peak bloom, so of course I couldn't join in*

*the jollies, the waist-to-waist dancing under lanterngloom
like moussed pumpkin. I was stuck home, sneezing. But afar
as binoculars could see, I'd watch the girls, the deep pumpernickel
of their throats when some lanky so & so spoke to them
in a velveteen drawl. Envy isn't a sturdy enough word. I was
a beaten path. But verily there's no way*

*around making a living. & I've never known sulking
to put any beans on your table. Given how damn
flammable I was, it took a lot of trial & error
to settle on a trade: I was a farrier until the day too much
haunch dander blinded me & a spooked hoof
ruined my hands. Then I worked as a greeter*

*at the bingo shanty, but the vast blabber
sprained my voice. The owner said I spoke
too dusky & showed me the exit.* Downcast, I even went
northwest to do time in a ball-bearing factory, *& again
the noise was artless
spite to my ears. But, through all this, I never got any relief

from the government. That's a thing I'm proud to say. I've
a few malingerers in my back-catalogue, & on their spirits
it was the mark of Cain. Inveterate job shuckers. Men
given any & all latitude to forge something
of themselves, but ever frittering it away. Not me. I didn't
intend to skulk through this life

infrastructureless. & pard, that's why I'm darkening
your door this fateful morn.* After speaking, he taxed
his hanky with a wheeze, then another. *Ah
drat,* he said. *Anyways, let me unspool something for you—*
his face was the quintessential
khaki of a toiler, & about his mouth the talk lines crinkled

corduroy—*I'm here porchside with an opportunity that's pretty
much tantamount to the skeleton
key for all of life's quarrelsome deadbolts.* His outfit
was loud: sunburst shirt, suspenders
in the tackiest magenta, & on his head this porkpie cap
shapeless as a feedbag. *I mentioned the mighty

work it took to find my calling. Decades I studied
after it. But snaking was the way. That long flummox
paid dividends, though. & now proudly I dub myself a professor
of self-betterment. Frankly,* he graveled, *I was put here
today to help you answer this question: are you yourself
incarnate? Have you jimmied the stubborn lock*

*on your potential? It was Pepin the Short or somebody
of his lofty ilk who said "don't you dare
act squirrely, son. Walk tall." & brother, for just a few months
of larder & lodging, I'll clue you in to this & more. I've bespoke
programs to help you manifest greatness. To talk shop
with the sacred. Shit, I'll even show you how to become immortal*

& then die. Before I could speak, he ferreted
past me, surveyed my place. *Gee oh. These digs'll do
swimmingly.* Then he wrestled off his boots, emptied
his marsupial pockets on my nightstand. *Give me a blink
to rejuice my batteries, & we'll strictly lay into it.* Onto my bed
he idled. Crimped his cap into a blindfold. I went outside, paced

the drear grounds in befuddlement. But, even at the most lonesome
corner of my property, I could still hear him snoring.
Sniffling.

The Coalblacked Jacobins

*How's things? Wish I could say fair
to middling. But it's devil take the hindmost of us, seems like.* A stringy
phalanx of union men abreast the highwall. Pitched above this coup-talk,
there is a Victrola keen—in May at the mouth of a seam even the gnats
are politicking. *Ah buddy,* another says, *I stay glancing up antsy
like an ACME safe might flatten me.* This coolish morning, there is
a handsome dividend of phlegm, throats frycooking. *Wish we had one
of them strike rats size of a parade float.* Laughing like an old diesel
berserk to turn over. Directly, a solstice blue Cadillac pulls in, tires
louchely chawing earth. Out steps a man sloughed in Sunday
best—sport jacket, veal-skin boots, tie patterned
gamecock. His neck is redcut, razored flab. Palmfuls
of smellgood like it's Election Day. The contrast between these men
is beyond smirking. It's a ballpeen to the schnoz. Bags fisticuffing
under each eye, every morning the worker finds his clothes
scarecrowing bedposts. Chemically wizened, the fabric works him
into its crosshatch, its denim rictus. By lunchbreak
it's cumbersome as plate. But well-liveried comes the land manager.
Now there's the gang that couldn't shoot straight. He's met with mule
plain faces. *Don't you boys know that shyness & rudeness
are first cousins?* A few toe sheepish at the silt. But one legs forward,
sunburnt, & says *here's your what-for: we're plumb herniated
from carrying this outfit. & I don't aim to keep pickaxing
years off my life so some Philadelphian's daughter can get college
learnt & trot around in jodhpurs. I want my due.* The land agent grins
telltale, stance askance, & eyes off into the muddled lapis, the fog
like unguent on the ridgetops. Fingers baroque with ore, he is as in
pigshit a truffle. *Two things: you boys ain't gonna slow down the Black
Jefe; that's like keeping an asteroid in first gear. & second, they'll be
no spielman here today to pencil you valiant. Just a motley few
doing without pay.* Coma-calm, he packs his lip. *Now who wants to
get down in that mine & hustle for me?* They're wellnigh buffaloed.
The truth is going down jagged, like bad Benadryl. All but the young
bantam. He makes to have ahold of the land manager. But two men
proportioned like oil derricks unfold from the Cadillac & are on him

with mace & axe handles. Soon he is turnipcolored. Tobacco spit
jetting from his mouth, the land agent says *gentlemen, I'm
scuff-proof*. Concurrent, a shift change—a detachment of scabs
coming out of Sheol. They trudge to the washhouse to sop off
the charnel. *Looks like the next batch of carts is primed; smartmoney
says you fellars oughta be aboard.* At their feet, the boy is leaking
rosewater. The land agent dusts his chinos all squirely & skeeters
of grit sublet the carcass. That instant, the younger men take back
their burdens. Droning off, forlorn by numbers, they're an assembly
line of spare parts. Now who remains fast at the picket but elderly
men with faces glyphlike against the detonated noon? *I believe
that's that.* The land agent & his two truncheons turn to go. But, mid
amble, he turns back & says *now when we drive off, keep your eyes
on these old artifacts. What they'll be doing is what the Good Book
calls coveting.* & truly, the old men's eyes were Roman
Cement on the taillights of the Cadillac. But what else is there?

That type: for nothing they'll put a molten one in your brain, invoice
your widow for the bullet. It's gotten where you can't afford to make
a fist. & arthritic as they are, you couldn't even swing one
in installments. So as the Cadillac peels out, slinging
plebeian gravel, all the old men can do
is wring the neck of the rooster
tail that's left in its wake.

A Country Horse-Doctor

It's the peregrine hour when all those who the day
demands something from are bracing
for it. At the pharmacy counter, the constable's tie is already
argyled in sausage gravy. & there's a liquor smirch
on the trifling briefs the magistrate didn't get
around to last night (but hellfire he will still
adjudicate them come petty claims court). Snow is on the ground
maggot-white, & the shop windows are chintzy
with sleet. But still there is this tumbleweeding

of the heart. If our county were any bigger
than a sitcom set, they would all herd lemminglike into the rough
spun monochrome of gas stations, outlet malls, & plyboard huts
where you can rent VHS tapes
rewound by mice & silverfish. Instead
most are at home, huddled up against the anachronism
of a woodstove, losing the staring match
to their oatmeal. But I don't have much
in the way of pathos for them. I was dogged

out of a dream hours ago by a man who said he'd blueblacked
his shins wading in a nightshirt through two miles of January
to the handiest phone. His Walking Horse
was in a pitiable way. So, jaw set, I went. I did a siege
time defrost—just cleared a murderhole's worth
of sight—& within a cigarette I was dreaming again about the white
flour of my wife's thighs, the dark between them
warm as fission. But my tires went over the municipal salt
like someone eating ice, & it made me stay

froggy. I held fast through the long gray caterwaul. They were gathered
hat-in-hand mournful around the horses' shanty. Greetingless, I saw
to its teeth, breast & rearmost quarter. But nowhere could I
find anything gone sideward—the horse just lagged there, stalactites
of cold coming off its nostrils, chuffing
raw cosmos. I asked what the matter was. They pussyfooted.

One finally said *we think she ate a pint bottle*. I looked at them
like that was routine. *You think? Why,* another said, *Jasper there
tuckered over in its stall around 10 with a glass pint in his shirtpocket*

& when I came up on him it wasn't nowhere findable. The third man,
Jasper, I wagered, had some mortifications on his face & was less
a canine from getting the everloving piss clapped out of him. So
there he mooned, altogether woo-woo from their unchurched
amends. *Well, you all'll have to watch her over this next day & see
if she grubs like usual & if her bowels are moving. It's kindly strange
that she'd pay any mind to a glass bottle, let alone gobble it. But
if she did there'll be an obstruction & that can get vicious. Odds are
your pint will turn up.* Those three just stared at me—men so beggared

that citified ducks would throw bread at them—until one said
we'd rather you just go ahead & dig around after it. They were trigger
happy. & I knew if I didn't do the doctoring myself, they would
vivisect the poor thing. My toolkit, frosted through, made an accordion
yap coming open. But the horse didn't shy or quail when I came
with the needle, the fluid stupor. & in the quell before
insentience, its face was a plaster ruin. I wanted to ease into her
with diplomacy, not parse her guts like they were so much

paperwork. So for a grizzly while, I was ungloved & civil-fingered—
the three men piled behind me in skunk-breathed expectance. &, as is
wont for farce, I found it there at the mouth of the wombholler.
I couldn't believe how smartly it was wedged, swaddled
in hormones, so there was no mutiny among the organs. Fairytale
snug, I didn't even want to take the forceps to it. But I did, &
salved & gauzed her shut. She slept like a newlywed. I gave
the men the pint, tinseled in afterbirth, & they made Christmas
faces—it was mostway full. They each took out a novelty

shot glass & poured it brim-high. This was too intimate
to watch, like seeing someone honor a *Do Not
Resuscitate*, so I turned to leave, knowing they hadn't any means
of paying up. But, wordless, to me

they tithed those first three shots. What can a man do
but slug them down, shake their hands? I stepped
out into the morning ruthlessly
lucid.

An Undeclared Farmer, Middle Creek, Kentucky, 1862

There's gunfire at queer hours. & some novice
sawing away at a violin. In this blank room with all
the wicks snuffed, in a churchly voice, my woman asks
how much more gloating do you think they'll do? I wish

they bottled gall. Then I might enterprise out & ask him
what tune that is
he's mangling. But I know the dark blood is up
in every cadet, & I don't want to end up ornamenting

a pike. Earlier, Pharaoh just barely wormed in
past their outriders & he said they had three boys in almond
& gray lashed together on a single mule, briquettes
of coal in their mouths. They were gouging

fun at the so-called dash & élan of the rebs: mummering
like picturebook belles with their kerchiefs & grungy
snotcloths, saying in a hammed-up dialect how much they longed
for some scion of Dixie to ruffle their petticoats. On one of the boys

they found an old sepia print of a wife or steady. They took turns
with it in their breeches, against their reeking satchels. Pharaoh told me
they were driving after Marshall's bunch
of irregulars, who'd made it here in a full lather, to the tatters

of this valley, not far ahead. When finally they met it was a rout:
with the first salvo, Jim Garfield's regiment of blues thinned
their line emaciate, sent men malingering into the hills, the bright
yelping yonder. Marshall's corps, even the hardiest among them

pleurisied & rheumatic, gave way like a gallows door. Within the hour
all that weren't lamed or gangrenous flocked off. Garfield let his men
have carte blanche with the corpses, & they spent the afternoon
nosing through them—an unkindness of two-legged crows. Less than

a mile upcreek, we were girding ourselves. Some crawled into corn
cellars, but most waited: hung up the wash, had supper. That evening
Garfield's host came through. Long gaunt centipedes of them, with
the Confederate prisoners sleepwalking, fettered to the baggage train.

One man, gutshot, kept falling to his knees in the rutted mud
& each time a faded-blue overseer would thrum him & say *quit
your interloping*. Eventually, he took a notion to just crop the man
lifeless. But, in his vehemence, he spooked the horse & it kicked

him truly in the face. For a moment, the hostage was freezeframed
there, wearing in deep rouge a shoeprint smile that said *Property
of these United States of America*, before his whole countenance
caved & he was dragged structureless the rest of the way. In the stock

trampled square that fronted our few cabins, Garfield halted his troop
& started ultimatuming: *you lot come on out now.
We've got to make sure you aren't hiding any dissidents. Comply
& we won't harm a hair on you.* So, slowly, like larvae

molting, we showed ourselves, the soldiers making famished
eyes at the mothers & daughters. Then commenced the loot. After
they'd requisitioned the casks of white liquor, Garfield turned them
to go. & then turned back. He looked at my woman, at me. *She yours?*

I nodded. *Have her pull that sackcloth up over her head.* I gave him
a wary peek. *My boys have been a long time seeing anything
built like that. They've earned it.* He had his sidearm bared. *Don't
make me leave her lay.* So I nodded again & she did. Whistles

& hooting galore. *I swear,* Garfield said. *Much obliged.* They camped
that night in the valley, toasting one another with the local meld, &
by daybreak were gone to Piketon & then on to viscera & glory
at Shiloh. Decades later, before he was to be inaugurated, Garfield

commissioned a memoir of his wartime, & the hagiographers asked
him about that skirmish at Middle Creek. He hadn't thought on those

doings in years, he said, but the writer pressed. What was it like
parlaying with the hillfolk? *The mountaineer is, by nature,*

feral, he said. *So as we were sweeping their wattle-n-daub
villages, it was no rank shock to find brother abed
with sister, man congressing with farmbeast.* A while later, after
they'd moved on to sundry other topics, he said *you know, for all*

the rudeness & sloth of that place, their women really

do have an unlettered charm.

Rough Customer

My cousin was something of a dilettante
of madness. Skullduggery, onanism, shooting

    his surname into the quaintness
        of a chapel wall—he was always flirting

with crazy. More than once, I saw him cop a feel
of the livid

    wirework of an electric fence
        without flinch. Saw him egg

young holler boys into tasting the spitting
image of whipped cream—hen

    diarrhea. & with firecrackers, I saw him
        turn a bullfrog into gothic

rain. Adolescing with him
made Jack Link's

    out of my nerves. In late teenhood, he took work
        muling pills from South Florida to London,

Kentucky. Tooling between states in a Buick
with *Bad Hombre* plates, he coined himself the famous

    wraith of Route 75. He did it until he had the folding
        money not to. After eight months of that

desperado stuff, he came home. But directly
he blissed his makings away, spent the rest

    of the year in a grinning
        dopefog. Then on, he just wheedled by

on the sturdy
samaritanship of his kin. Every so often

    though, to cut through the narcotic
        dinge, he'd try his hand at something new. Dumping

coal slurry in the incoordinate dark, digging
grave after grave

    just for the cold drinks, & putting pneumatic
        divots in a calf's skull

on the kill line. He worked some as a farrier
just to make sure the mares were clipped

    to the quick, left limping
        along on petals

of abscessed tendon. He ruined many
a fine-blooded gait. Finally, they put him away

    for leaving three trailers
        half-arsoned. A fire marshal asked him what

happened & he said *I'm not sure, maybe the insurance
wire got too hot,* winked. That was over a decade ago. The other

    morning, I was on my way someplace & saw two boys playing
        with a downed power line

& I thought of him. His phlegmy heart. Paroled,
he didn't make any tracks back here. None of us

    heard from him, & haven't since. Not too many
        months past, though, somebody in the know

told me that he'd taken up
a Pentecostal ministry. That he was preaching

      to a fanatic 200 every Sunday. Word is, he said he had to
            forswear us every one. Anymore, he couldn't condone

our wrongdoings. I can just see him
up at the pulpit, wringing the hell

      out of that holy alphabet. & I can see the gleeful
            ick in his eyes when it's time to baptize

the penitents. I know he loves getting to hold them
underwater, slobbers for those few seconds

      between drowning
           & deliverance.

Pastoral vs. Georgic

*"What separates a georgic from a pastoral
is work. In a georgic, there's no denying
that work is being done."*
—Thomas Haddox

My head is a grassy church. There is sun-nuzzled wash on the line
outside the parsonage. Songbirds are heart on heart in the fatherly
arms of an alder, but those hosannas you hear are not
their ambiencing. It's just the villeins absolutely obliged to their twilight

vespers. It is indeed the choicest shank
of the evening, & these endearingly snub-nosed folk in cordwood
slippers & flaccid hats are not kissing
cousins to dysentery & scrofula. There is no high

plight, & not a soul is going steady
with jeopardy. On the brambled verandas—sipping lemon cordial,
dandelion & burdock—the gentry are of even temper. Their savorsome
inhaling is not troubled by the downwind cheddar of abattoirs or cattle

in deep earthturning heat. Upholstered in the humid oblique
of night coming on, they don't pay any care to their tenants
hoofing home. & what of those swagbacked Atlases, shouldering
the whole? The ebb of their talk is so wormbent it's loveable, a little

boy sorely missing his front teeth. They are in peak spirits, pudgegutted,
pinky-nailing the comeuppance from between their own like it's daily
bread. It might edge off chill, but that doesn't matter—they're shawled
in contentment. Their feet in clogs are brute as pumice, but still they go

buoyant through the night. & it's complete & final black, but they're not
wayward in this dark. Raw grace enunciates their going. These mud
husbanders, they know there's no cause to doggone
their betters. After all, this flesh is something

        we're only pilgrim to.

I am half-batty to be among them. If I say it, it's so. I am there. I am
in jinxed tandem with the least of them. & I'd be grateful to forever
midwife a plow through unversed dirt—to just go on breaking
fetal ground—or wear like a sumptuous doublet an armload

of bees from the hives of my seigneur. Yes, that is an era
I'd be merry to stumble onto. Regardless, I'll tell you where I'm not:
I'm not up to my wishbones in this dishwater
dawn, trying to shepherd with spade & prybar a D-8 bulldozer

back into flock on this mountainside slathered
in disagreeable weather. My old man does not look like a cosmonaut
in his blowtorch gown. He is not strapped haplessly into the cockpit
of *Kapital*, trying to rile the starter. The rank tension of jobs undone

isn't warbling his neck, shuffling his jowls, like he just entered
orbit. He didn't just bawl me out, both barrels, for sagging the flashlight.
& surely I am not so soft-witted that I still offer my neophyte advice.
He doesn't have to keep saying *I'm shearing this goat, you just*

hold its head, & at dusk, we won't slink home, refugees
from success, in the same gruel-light. We won't be so hangdog ashamed
that we scald the work off before quaking the threshold; we will not
blight ourselves to the elbow with lye. & unlike something in the back

room of a bad dream, my granddad will not be there swapping skin
for recliner felt. He is not in breakneck wilt, too much popcorn
lung to fog a mirror, & I won't have to take shiving drags off a Winston
& pipe the smoke down the swollen ductwork

of his throat. My father doesn't steer
clear of us like an EPA audit. We are not just cellmates in this
singlewide. & nobody, not a blessed one of us, will risk a glance
at the competition grade skeet-gun mounted above the furnace

         above all else.

The Selected Works of Judas Iscariot

*Now we're all waterlogged
Baptists here, so none of that
postmodern stuff. Just learn
us what's making the boy act oblong.* While speaking, the principal never
looks up from his bologna sandwich. This disinterest is spelled out

by his Fu Manchu of mustard & jus. Heimliched by gust & downpour,
the blousefront of the counselor is steeply rumpled. She quits the office
without gussying herself, leaves behind footsteps
in a sopping fluer-de-lis. The lowdown: she is from Saint Paul, a Peace
Corps mendicant, deployed to Kentucky on grant. What she is after

is forgiveness for her loans. She has a bachelors in Psychology, &
that's good enough to shrink heads in this district. But all she did early
on was fret the woodfungus off her desk with the heavenmost point
of a crucifix that wouldn't stop bowing its nail. Finally, her first: a boy
named Judas Iscariot Jacobs. Word was, his father gave the name

to let him know from the nonce that he had sin enough on the pearly
ledgers to never get anywhere
near square. In disposition, he'd always waxed bizarre—he didn't walk
until the age of 12, his elder brothers just yakking him around
on their haunches, & if asked why he'd say no one ever bothered

to teach him proper. But of a sudden he'd taken to silence. Six months
devoutly mute. Last week, to beat it all, he was in remedial
gym when the coach decided he'd had a bellyful of the boy's quiet
truancy, aiming to cow him in front of the others. *Speak up
if you're any kind of man,* said Coach. Judas simply motioned

for pencil & paper, scratched something: *that hair on your chest
is just a toupee.* & now, étouffée of sweat & eagerness in the crockpot
her palms make, she waits for him. Instantly, she can tell he isn't long
among the upright. At their joinings, his limbs
are too lenient, chopper-blading all directions

but cardinal. He sits down like someone unkinking
a colostomy bag. She begins with niceties, the performative
saccharines highbrows use to flavor
the bite out of what they're after. An hour into it,
& he's still got that face on. Bland

as leek broth. Instinctually, she reaches him some scraps
of paper. Two caterpillar back. The first: *you're the type to remind me
of my table manners during a famine.* The second says only
talk bald. At dismissal, epochs later, she goes heavyhearted
to the principal. *He spoke once, but I still recommend a Special

Ed evaluation. There are egregious developmental delays. He couldn't
answer the most straightforward question off my template.*
The principal says *hold your horses. Let's me & you give him another
whack before we bugle after the bureaucrats. They're always skunking
things up. Besides, we're one sentence to the better. Way I spy it,

progress is more atribe to a squirt gun than a pressure washer.* So
at morning bell, in a classroom of gulag brick, they batter him
with questions avant-garde to anal. His vegetableness abides. By lunch,
the knot in the principal's necktie is lasso-slack. *I never claimed to be
Mr. Sophistication,* he says, *but your questions would have me figuring

on my fingers & toes.* They are licking wounds in a utility closet. *Shelve
that bunk: ask claws-out the same thing that got him talking yesterday.
What are the four seasons?* came out of her mouth before the hinges
hushed. *That's kindergarten stuff,* Judas says: *squirrel, deer, rabbit,
& turkey.* The atrophy in his voice is like hoax nails

on a blackboard. After a tall second, the principal says *scurry back
to class, Judas. We're done & field-dressed here. What a crime
it would've been to loose the whitecoats on him,* the principal says.
You can't be serious. The counselor's face is an oil portrait
by some stern & penniless Netherlander

of exasperation. *He is clinically unwell; he needs a psychiatric renaissance. What that boy needs is an old wiseman to pitch his tree stand, doctor his rifle.* The principal is bushwhacking the flak from his indexnail with a free lunch voucher. *He might not speak frequent, but when he does talk he talks plain sense.*

Present Tense Timeless

That there's the wrath of the lamb. That's what Boo said every AM
after backsliding. He said this duly to himself, but I heard it
through the bathroom wall no suppler
than looseleaf. After a night of drinking, there'd be this dark

nativity in his bowels, the colon
asphalted with poor decisions. & for hours he'd struggle to leave
something in the toilet that looked like inclement sky. I remember
his sheets, nunwhite & gnarled. I remember him crazily

pleating the shadows, praying in sleep he hadn't turned
those sheets drab with flux. Finally, thick into morning, he'd come out
like a breechbirth. & for a week or thereabout, he'd make a Tao
out of teetotaling. But for him, each time, this was more than just

the cult of Self-Serenity—his own granddaddy died drinking
canned heat in the depression (the family crest should've been a liver
hobnailed). I'd always heard tell that Boo favored him in both jawbone
& temperament. It was all anecdote, though; there were no pictures.

His grandmother believed any likeness was a heresy. But Boo's father
did carry a few of the man's ponderings, plumbless as they were.
On being ammonia'd awake after a ten-day debauch, he had only this
to say: *West Kentucky—shit—out there it's so flat*

you can watch your dog run away for a week. Then for months
he spoke squat, just laid in the linen
overgrowth of his bed, fluorescing confettilike
with jaundice. But on a bitterly percolated morning

in the winter of 1939 he sat up
brine-eyed & said to his wife *God gives it back to us*
many-fold. & by the week's end, he had already descended
into wormhood. I know all that pickled ancestry

must've weighed on Boo like Imodium those mornings
he was so desperate to leaven out. To be any other way
than what seemed gene-writ. But quartz
mouthed, he'd battle free of the washroom, come to lull

on the windowsill, & spark two beeswax candles.
Lit, the smoke would come off them
in cursive. & all naked
nerves, he'd stare out the window at the long puce scarves

of dust tarping the coal tipple. & like this, his face
acryliced in place, the day flickered to dreg. In the 8pm sallowness,
at the last anemia of the candles, he'd go to his miniature fridge,
come back with fifths akimbo. After a deep glug, he'd say *tonight*

you just can't let me take the Lord's exalted name
in all sorts of vain. So I'd spend the night watching him do just that.
What does he expect—that I'll just cut capers in these chains? That I
won't take names, take what ought to be mine from this benastied

world? No, he's dead certain that I'll not do a thing but grin & say
please slop me with a second-helping. & here's the dismal
fact: If I was liquid enough to be a betting man, I'd put my wampum
on him. I'll like as not stay neighborly, just mind this hurt

the way it's been done since times fireless, the way I'm doing
my utmost to now. By then, he'd be all but interred. & just before
yellowing out, he'd say something
in chalk-lipped summation: *what I can promise you*

is that, for all the teeth-gnashing & soul-auditing I've done, God has
not indemned me against anything. Not one homeless thing. All this,
ad nauseam. It was a hardwearing clemency I had for Boo. I couldn't
stay surly at him. Couldn't ever blame him for believing this life

was gypsied against him. & years later, when he was found daggered
to the hard vein—in the bluing ides of an overdose—I didn't resent
that either. I knew it'd be un-understood. That they'd call it
a civic lapse, a disordered act. To me it was textbook

orthodoxy. I've always known men like that. They're obsessed
with getting all the ham off the riblet. They'll tonguelash the plasma,
tweeze the last drops out of a bottle. At birth, satisfaction leaves them
in a cradle on the orphanage doorstep.

All Assurances, This Was South

of anywhere you'd rather be. A muller of shake & bake meth
by vocation, I was prospecting town to town, all variations of the same
spittoon, for Sudafed when I saw the sign: *Welcome
to Eufala, Alabama. You are now just 6652 miles from Calvary.* I still
can't arithmetic why, but then & there I nearly aged out

of the Anthropocene. Eyes olden with rain, I saw an apparition
of myself, or someone else godforsaken as me, 200 years previous. He
was riven from the sweet Kahlúa of corncrib shadow, taken by buggy
to a field widowed of cotton. Out of casketpine & Cajun boudoirs
the homeguard rigged a gibbet. Indictments were read against him.

In black type he was codified a craven, layabout. No last
rites. Then the fizz of rope, his neck printed
animal in the Alabama sun. All at once, I was in a Meat & 3.
Hamsteak on my plate looking ripe
for biopsy. A waitress, mostly gristle, came by to top me

off with prune juice of questionable vintage. The tablecloth bulged
vittles, but such hospitality was a lapband round my appetite. Manic, I
fled to the town square, but kept meeting people with white picket fences
for teeth. Campaign signs for smiles. On my neck there was a creeping
dew. No matter how busy my stride, I couldn't get beyond the damnable

kitsch of storefronts, display windows syruped
in Stars & Bars, Simply Southern. In the wallglass I could see myself
irradiated, ill-lit. Could feel my pupils dribbling out
haphazard against cheeks, chin. I was haywire. I was hell. In gasping
lieu of lithium, I imagined what I imagine New England

must be like: the colonial gloam
of storefronts, a tasteful necklace of lamplight on
Main Street. & of course a moon
you could spread on sourdough. No luck sipping on this
fugue like stovewarm manna though, cause I was being fanged

ditzy by the blonde noon leaving me
its fever, my face red as watermelon meat. I kept the pace
thoroughgoing though, fudge it all. & on the sacks of fertilizer & spent
two liters in the bed of my truck I went
primeval. Exiling so much of this I could actually see the end

stage vitiligo of the base metal. But it ran
comely. & soon enough I smelled the trees
of render & carrion out behind the Tyson plant at the town's most
tousled fringe. Finally mild, for the thousandth time I charted
my stars toward a new life: trek northeast, man a village

grocer in Massachusetts—fishing trowelfuls of rock candy
from the barrel for the boarding school snivelers—or keep the hedge
rows regal at one of those cliff-clinging manses in Newport, Rhode
Island. For that moment, I was astral. But, hours drudging
through the green liminal, I had time to think

on the work I'd done that day, the work I'd avoided: anything
gainful. I believe in clock-punching about like my grandfather did
after he got laid up & off by the coal mines. *Well I might strike
a lick again someday but I ain't a glutton for it.* He said this
a month before his heart blew out like preserves

canned all harebrain. Driving, that wisdom was a cicada
in my ear, a twinge of glare in the rearview. & I must've let this
blot me out, because next I knew I was in Mobile, on a pier
orphaned of all—commerce, camaraderie—but the water
chafing its shins, the air so dopily histamined. & the mucus

on the Gulf that night was synecdoche for decay
the CSA over. Gracious God how I tried
to point my jalopy true north, but time
& again my tears—same as those bleaters
in off-white & butternut—spoiled my aim.

A Day Laborer Dreams Away His Drive Home

I want to read the love lines
        in your blackwatch plaid
              & kiss the cracks
                      in your hard hat

like a snake
        tongues the hatchlings
              in their coop—an old swing set
                      dressed in rust & guy-wire.

No I don't care a bit to change
        tonight's half-baked channel
              cat to tenderloin or a pillowy chop
                      just please let me watch you drink

up the throwaway slushings
        of pan lard. I want you to lust
              after my leftovers. I don't mind
                      to mince words: let me take

your aching feet out of those boots
        & massage them like I'm casing
              sausage or pin-rolling dough. Go ahead
                      & get comfortable. I have nothing

to say about the automatic dishwasher
        you never got me, or the rain gutter
              garroted with leaves, or the toilet seat
                      birthmarked green & brown. I'll serve you

iced-tea with a few broken fingers
        of bourbon. I'll help you savor this final day
              of free-trial satellite. & later in bed
                      I might even make you steal

some of my beauty
      sleep. This time
            I might even leave
                  the light on.

Sonnet for the Preachiest Loop in My Belt

Round midnight
the plushbellied men—their vitals
fetched up in flak jackets
of saturated fat—shrink cold-footed
into the pantry to make sandwiches
out of sidemeat & snotty aioli.

In the gaunt hills
a wolf—his muzzle done up
bloodmuddy from the moon
sweetened bowels of an old kill—hears
a lovemate croon
in cross-eyed hunger
& has naught to say
for himself.

We Still Kill the Old Way

What a fateful contraption, the body. There are reckonings
performed in the inner ear to keep you upright, exorcisms
done to stop the cells from sickling, the blood
from petering out. It must be forensically
scrupled. & in its functions it abides

a friar's one-mindedness. But there is also marvelment—God
in the means of production. It intuits: no one has to teach you to read
the braille of the nipple. & breezy we learn to sign the lingo of the hard
of hearing. A man could tell you tungstenfaced *I'm not fat*
I'm tactically wide & you wouldn't need to draw out the blood

pressure cuff to figure his truthfulness. You'd just see it
in the way he has his pants torqued on. & even the measliest of us
is his own paterfamilias—every fart confected in-house. There is no need
for prescription hirelings to muck out the dogtrot
that runs from diaphragm to rectum. Kidneys, gallbladder: these deal

with the impishness of uric acid, render it
aloof & alkaline. But the soul is no custodian. On occasion you'll file
a quitclaim, deed yourself to others. & they'll do you like those pages
from the New International Bible with the daylights
pinched out of them. In havoc, they'll garrison you. But after the peace

has been sued for, the trebuchets razed for banquet tables, they'll make off
with everything that's not hammered down. & liegeless you'll be left
to repatriate, tasked with selfcraft from the floorboards
up. & the delegates that come to congress with you will be Heaven
Hill, sweet-tar cigarillos, & foodstuffs all powdered

& pestilent. Until some afternoon you waken &
within your skull there is a trampling
like Exodus. You pull down the sheets & see your legs
kudzued with varicose, your wife
beater ripped to tourniquets. & in your surrender

colored rags you'll gimp to the mirror, grimed over, & reckon
whether it's you or the lot of them that deserve credit
for this walking   Golgotha.

III

"Tradition is not the worship of ashes,
but the preservation of fire."
—Gustav Mahler

The Redneckery

Our national flower: an augur bit.
Our anthem? The occasional
clangs from a rip-roaring game
of horseshoes. & even though it violates
the Establishment Clause, blacking out
off Goldschlager & praying you barf
up a truck payment is our bonded
religion. I believe the seminarians
call that a Primitive
Baptist. & the poets tell of Magic
Mart bodice-rippers taking wing, flying
off the shelves. You'll surely find some
subterranean rage & the genial
menace of Gene Hackman in that
there $2 DVD bin. Our justice
of the peace is out in the parking lot, inspecting
his dipstick. Bearded
by long white yawns
of radiator smog, he's thinking
that the cure for all that ails us
is a Manwich & some Easy Mac. Too bad
he just blew a week's per diem on the spiffiest
pair of diabetes slippers this side of the I-
64 corridor. Honk twice if you think the Fiscal
Court ought to audit his embezzling ass. My great
grandpap was named Pharaoh, & he let
a lot of blood for this Egypt, this
puny bottomland. Warts & all, it's ours
outright. Owning free & clear the earth
you scourge is a hillbilly's *objet petit a*.
I've whittled most of my life away
in libraries, & even I know that
the red on our necks comes from those kerchiefs
at Blair Mountain. From the miners wearing red
to flex their solidarity with Red Labor

worldwide. Floor to ceiling deifications of Mother
Jones & Eugene Debs were with piety
hung in every winesink, every dogtrot. &
the lushes there, arm-in-arm, still sang
hotly of the Brothers Gracchi, their baritones
gruff with silicosis. & in the 70s, during the mine
wars, Harlan County kindergarteners gave up
pledging allegiance to the flag. Instead, they blared
"Which Side Are You On?" over the intercom system
at morning assembly & addressed their Christmas
wishlists to the union local. They trusted the UMWA
a hell of a sight more
than old Saint Nick & his team
of scab reindeer.

I hate fiddle music. I don't have a taste
for tater candy. & I'd rather pore over
Sanskrit in a cloistered abbey than blast
Tannerite on some bumfuck mountaintop. But
in the face of the targeted
enfreakment of everyone & thing
around me, these small disharmonies don't
pass muster. Eons of doing
without has led the Redneck to the bleeding
edge of decency.

This is about who gets to eat their fill
from the fat of the land. This is for anyone
who's ever punched &/or kissed me.

We Were Put on This Earth to Fart Around

It's official: I just well & truly slipped
my last disc. & in my left ear the tinnitus still
sounds like spastic math—data
recklessly collating. With each passing day I
kowtow a smidge more to the folk

physics of aging. Through the night there is wine
dark ache, & then the nervy thrill of waking & wondering
what will kneecap me today? Safe to say I can't
globetrot like I once could. I'll concede that
every day is a gift, but why

does it have to be a pair of socks? *Brón.* I never planned to
emote all over you. Gutwrench
after gutwrench, yet I am glad
to the brink of fear? Likely
in cahoots with the phone company, someone

someplace is just about to floor me
with a collect call. 90 godforsaken minutes
from New York to Paris. What a world. At a moment's
magick, I feel all the unsayable grumbles hounded
out of me by something daffy. A pulled finger. A stampede

of flatulence. My friend's cousin's dentist lost the better half
of his motor function to the corkscrewings
of a prion, but till the bedwetting end he ate
up all that was crass & grab-ass. *Now at least they can't
lock me in the penitentiary for palming a good nutritious hunk*

of woman, he'd say from his sickbed. & to his candy
striped butt-wipers: *you're a sight sightlier than my dental
hygienists were.* He'd motion low to the ground with his
weedwhacked hand & declare *I've practiced
dentistry since you were yay big, & you know I nearly*

think a root-canal beats working for a living. Thank
fuck I never have to do it again. Just reminding
myself of that tastes like Lobster Thermidor. Silver
linings & such. But lickety-split how we forget that
infinite growth is the logic of the cancer cell. That's why

almost every other week there are synchronized
swan dives out of the heavenscuffing windows
in Wall Street high rises. There's a lot of ruing
to go around about the state of my affairs, the cold
celestial shoulder, but I won't complain. Jobless, I walk

on gilded splinters. Back in our mother
country, my kinfolk were makers
of high trouble. They're the reason
that the Geneva Convention considers bagpipes
to be a weapon of war. Prayerfully, we've simmered down. Swords

into ploughshares & all that. But lo, I'll just never acculture
to selling my time. So maybe it's ire, old ire, that keeps me
here, me & my muscadine & my mulehead, farming
hemorrhoids on a loveseat that hasn't been re-cushioned
since Bonnie Prince Charlie went kaput. But isn't it prettier

to imagine me the last yeoman? To believe I'm barnstorming
against the workaday, the small-souled & the cow-eyed. That,
screening this Michael Mann movie about the safecracker who can't
jimmy open his own heart, I am planting some kind of flag, making
the most of one matchless hour, over & again. There's no need

for a newfangled program. Just quotidian mud. Just me
       to the Achilles' in it, waging
              my cornpone jihad.

Elegy for JOANN Fabrics

As we speak, private
equity is getting the last shred of tenderloin

off the bone. Their spreadsheets & algorithms cut
cleaner than any oncologist. I'm talking margins

that'd make a CyberKnife blush. *Grandmas are supposed to
knit & work needle*—according to a jowly man in the Facebook

comment corral—*now they just laze around & watch
pimple-popping highlight reels. Thanks, feminism!! Crying

shame,* another man laments. *That store always smelled
like those candies old church ladies kept

in their big kangaroo-pouch purses. Takes me right back
to way back when.* Midst this hypertensive talk

of handheld brains & global gubbermint conspiracy, I'm
thinking of the jobs lost, of the kitchen table

come-to-Jesus moments that are looming
in Greater Flyoverville. Of missed rent & the bite of that COBRA

premium. It's more or less the same tired story: communities
gone hardscrabble. Cars up on cinderblock. More people

know the going price of scrap than starting
wages at that ghosted battery plant. A constitutional Right

to Work state, by god. Coal miner, roughneck, lint
head—all made redundant, rarefied as the dodo. & now

the bell tolls for the JOANN Fabrics *team member.* All in
a day's creative destruction. But me, I'm an optimist. Always

look on the bright side: those superstore
layoffs have more time for their hobbies. Listening

to Dave Ramsey while they drive Uber. Learning
to code, grind crypto, or maybe even

crochet.

Lastward

In the nursing home I was once
overing my papers
one more time: husbanding
the correspondence, diaries, & shaggy
miscellany into something
sage. In youth & young manhood, middle
age, I was an academic of the dead
languages. Latin, Esperanto, I gave
bulky lectures. I could make a single, lordly yawn
last the class period. My students, at this college of striving
kulaks, were daresome to tell me
that the hour had passed. It was almost time

for pudding & pills, & the ragged welding
of my own cursive started
to make my eyes run
tepid. I thought O dear: these
are the motheaten, back-attic ruminations of a man
in wane. Where is the bloodthrum, the red
yawp? With sprained vision, I went over
them again—each letter, a little
kinked corpse. Of a sudden, I was palsied
by doubt. The orderlies had to tote me
to my communal table for snack. & as I sat
there, envying the thick skin

on my tapioca, the uncertainty started
to go through me
like an intestinal virus. What of my sole
tome? If these long shepherded
logs of mine, which I'd hoped might give
scope & bookend
to my twilight, just amounted to the lax
sphincterings of the bedridden, then what
of my spindly oeuvre? The only book
I'd published: a study of the yearning

syrup of the Appalachian idiom. It aimed
to atomize every hair
trigger utterance. To encompass all
the rawboned poise. Some doleful critic called it
flabby. & I'll admit it had some undue
heft, stretch marks
from all the chitlin & frybread
fed musing. But I wanted it to give the whole
motion: the charred kinesis of a coon
hunt at midnight—hounds with fetus-colored tongues
aloll, men whoop-drunk
around a campflame—& the ceaseless power

& telephone wire strung pole to pole
like wonky sutures. The cankered
poetry they relay. Squinting back through
my uncollected work, it dawned on me
what's absent: the judgeless
tangle of hick talk. It's all gone
nasal. Dull & unsalted—a rhetorical
casserole. If you went by the
bromides in my journal, the decade
prior was just regimented
languish. Ten dim years through
lined only by the funk

of bedsore salve, bureaucratically approved
mush. Studying *haught*, I'd lost all contact
with the ardenthearted. In that cafeteria, I realized
I was in the foggiest hills
of enfeeblement. Soon, I'd be vacant
minded, a gurgling nag
of bones. Then & there, at a table
full of professional droolers, I decided I wanted to go out
doing something un-annullable. To use the last morsel
of my wits…getting senseless. That night, after sleeptime
medicine, I crept to the home's dingiest wing—

where they boarded the wards
of the county. I woke Stacy, a short-winded
indigent from Lookout Mountain who fermented
busthead hooch in his handicap
friendly commode. He came to
gape-lipped, awry of larynx, breathing red
static. His lungs sounded
soldered. But there was this nutty welling
of tears at the corner
of his crow's feet when he saw the two softshell
packs of Winston Lights I had. Next morning, at shift
change, in the backmost common room, the aides

found a duo in Daniel
Boone costumes, the snoring
coals of a fire upkept with pages
from peer-reviewed journals. Half
a blackened pet rabbit billowing
from a greenwood spit. & *Sweet
Ruination* written in thumbtacks on the corkboard
amongst the lunch menus & bingo digest. The coroner
said that those two graybeards died of a hangover
that ought to be hanging in a museum.

Psalm to Be Spoken in a Hill's Ribcage, Where the Heart Ought Be

All hours, they are clomping through sluice
that's shoe-mouth deep. & with them totemic the little lilies
of blister & slough floating   Zen
in their boots. But getting from A to B, coal vein to conveyor, on feet
turned Styrofoam is the paltriest of their worries. There are cairns
down here that an Egyptologist couldn't excavate, let alone those
cardboard cutouts at OSHA. & there're whole wiffleball rosters of men
who one dawn jittered into the gall bile of this mine & come quitting-
dark never surfaced. Gone so long their common law spouse is named
Rubble. & behind they leave women whose only recompense
is a company ham each Christmas, some tattered & hand-me-down
condolences from the foreman when he chances by that house
with the gutters ramshackling off like a '70s hairdo—a litter
of children, all runts, in the yard pretending that the hoecake
& Crisco they're jawing on are   smooches
of Hershey. But this crew is extant, swinging mattocks. For quorum
there's the nerve-doping jar, biceps fuzzy as bad analog, of bladepeaks
clacking against bubonic zinc. Only trace amounts of that
chewy idiom. Mostly men looking   old
testament at each other. Like that water torture they're doing
dissertations on in the Orient, the stalactites   slobber
on them immemorial. Gloveless, their palms are fractal & cratered
as doomed moons. They'll soldier on like this, artisans
of the callous, till it's time to leave things for the mausoleum
shift, who'll probably be damned as well
to ascend   into the unhomely
brine of 6am.

Truly, what necromances these men
off their scrawny bedsteads each morning, takes them down
into the deviled pitch? I'll flat tell you: it's the chirp
of eggs in a skillet, mothers   bitching
into their toddler's earache. Homespun quilts
of gravy on your catheads. A pup neurasthenic from table

skimmings. That leisurely poached cabbage smell
of thrombosis stockings airing out over every vent. The jaundiced
newborn put to candy in blunt sun. & each does it
for the other, of course: that miner beside him made
Dalmatian by coal spume. Even Levon—the Armenian who fled
Ataturk's malignant pen—always beaming lopsided & saying *how
do you are?* Brought-on or not, they respect him because he works
like Hephaestus. Heaping coal & never once   begging
off because *gahdang I tweaked my shit-chute* or *my good lung
is a mummied fig*. Above ground, they rib him for the hifalutin
beading on his skull cap, the baklava in his lunch pail. They take
as sacrosanct his Istanbul yarns. Listen cross-legged
like schoolchaps. They all laugh out   black
chaff at his mimings of them, their puzzling diction. They have
him over for supper & for their fidgety kids
he is Kubla Khan, scimitar up, loping into Damascus. He plays
a mean horselord. Even the parents—puddled into wicker
rockers, worn slap out—can't conquer a grin. & that rarefied smile
of Levon's is chronic. Underground, even. & when they find him
whey-faced from too much methane, he'll still be grinning
neon & neighborly as a vacancy sign. For now, though, things are just
so. Down there, it's dim enough that the miners have all learned to see
in sepia. To not wallop each other in the teeth
chattering sanguine. But occasionally Levon, pale
as a geisha, steps into the pilsner
of another's headlamp   & nods.

Blue Yodel for Back When

In Savannah, I don't have a single issue
keeping my kilter on these speedways
& switchbacks that General Oglethorpe so painstakingly
cobbled. How orderly the earth is here—due kudos

to the debt peons who actually evened it. What tonic it is
to my feet: this pavement without burl, fissure, or chewing
gum psoriasis. & the out & out postbellum romance—
there's Confederate jasmine, climbing jessamine in moony

tryst with the café lattice. The water in commodes
is glacier-grade. Birdbath tranquil. Sheer homeostasis
has me motion sick. I see a teenager, maybe a wishful junior
varsity majorette, twirling her baton on a buzzcut lawn &

it makes my kneecaps jangle. The only thing I can do is look up
to all the local people with their PhDs
in scoffing. Among them must be the expertly
anal engineer who superintends all this. Who keeps the trolleys

& rickshaws at a cogent thrum, dresses down
any analog clock that doesn't appreciate daylight
savings time. Even in the thick of this reconstructed
Dixie, with its every i dotted & t crossed, I still can't get the best

of my wayfaring thoughts. Out of the hinterlands
of memory comes my uncle, the Kentucky draughtsman. Pincered
between his thumb & ringfinger, a mouthwash cup of Scotch
cut with Pepto-Bismol. He is nursing this, telling whoppers. He

hams up his time as a land surveyor. Swears that on the first Monday
of each January, he was forced to layaway in a box car
with his theodolite & plumb bob, ride that freighter clear to Frankfort.
Tote his ignoble instruments to the capitol, square his calibrations

with theirs. Said the State Corps of Engineers termed this
The Hillbilly Pilgrimage on account of we hayseeds

from too far east of the bluegrass being a hazard
to property lines & public safety. Too numskull

to suss our own math. *In all fairness, I did
do an awful lot of guesstimating,* he said & showed his rickety
dentures. So toothsome, those stories. Every word went down
like birthday vittles. Even in this hypernormal city, with its marquees

graffitied by the names of so many concert pianists & C-suite
skinflints, naught ministers to me like that. Tell me why
it's solely the defeated I can put any faith in? Here, *lineage*
isn't much more than a word in the accursed writ of estate

tax legislation, a corn-fed billfold, but to me it means throats
clearing in the goosepimple light, work trucks coming to
in pruny black cold like someone speaking
with a beastly stammer. It means thieving

your living from sourpuss ground. Even from the rearmost porthole
of the paper mill, even with all that tannin in my eyes like burlap
cataracts, I can still see how storied it looks, the limelit
downtown. If I fix on it for too long everything goes to Miracle

Whip between my ears. What I need is hard
kilometers between here & me. That's why on my days off I'm still
up early, throttling inland. & I don't stop until there's some hitching
post, some irradiated gas station where the underbred &

muleheaded gather to bitch about the lard-free biscuits, the price
of mom & pop diesel. & more often than not I sit
a sort of vigil there till nearabout closing. By then, staying awake
is just woozy pugilism, & the radiator cooing diabolically

wholesome doesn't help. &, slogging home, there's always several
dumbstruck bucks that are hell-bent on eloping with the gloam
on the grill of my truck. But none of that matters—I'd pay Upper
West Side rent for a booth there if it meant the blindest

chance of hearing fourth or even
fifth-hand word of someone I've loved.

Those Old Chromosomes Were Known to Ramble

My mother's father was a fount
of cockeyed wisdom. Wooed by the far

flung & farther fetched, he left
my mother & her own sainted mother

in an ungentlemanly lurch. Said he was fishing
for dignified work. Something that wouldn't just

make ends meet, but knock
the socks clean off his naysayers. Instead

he spent the next quarter-century warming
the ache out of his hands at the trash fire of first one

& then another roustabout, wheeling & dealing
under that big arch in St. Louis. He held

a jester's court among the hyena
cackles of the hitchhikers, hoods, & scarcely

employed while his wife & children waited
in line for government cheese. He turned tail

when my mother was six, so her memories of him
are mostly acid-washed. But one sticks out

like a beachgoing albino: he was huddled over
the sink, pretending to do dishes. Every so often, he'd toss

a glance back at her in her highchair, pantomime
a rag across some crumb-spangled tableware, then peer

performatively around the corner of the alcoved kitchen
into the den. Her mother was out there battling

the landline. All this tomfooling sent my own mother
into a laughcry fit. Against the floor tile

her chair made wispy clatter. This mustn't have sat right
with her father, cause the clownlines on his face

all vanished. For some fruitcake reason, he held up
two pieces of fine china, padlocked his

eyes to hers, & let them sail. By the legs of her chair
they made landfall. In her haste, my mother's

mother got lassoed up in the phone cord, & laid
waste to a hunk of wall. *What on earth?* Her mother said, tripping

into the kitchen. Her father was already sweeping up
the commotion. *Why that girl there got a wild hair*

& started playing frisbee, he said. Stark
raving, my grandmother administered some frontier

justice for the first & last time in her life. Then tucked
my mother back in her highchair with a strawberry

rump. She bumbled back to the den all
flush-faced. & once again it was simply

father & daughter. Cozied up with them in the kitchen: burly
silence. The only sound was the ominous

plink of the faucet. Her father was throwing long
looks out the window overtop the sink. Through pinched

sobs, my mother could see his vast Jutland back
ciphering against cheap polyester. *Now little*

girl—he finally said, still ogling the windowglass—*there're just two keys to a successful life. The first: don't blab*

everything you know.

Swiftly Tilting Planet
after Krzysztof Kieślowski

The problem
with a poet's equilibrium: I keep falling
in love.

Cost of Living

Sunday. Some prosaic shopping. Egg whites,
Neosporin. Something that won't do

half bad in a Dutch oven. Leave out the spices
from Kashmir & St. Croix—they're too high

octane. Can't stand to upset your gut
flora. Scant traffic in the aisles, little chatter

or teem. Just gruesome reverb. One palsied wheel on a cart
complains through subwoofers. But the shelves…abject

plenty. I eye aubergines with queenly poise, a Golden
Delicious of esteemed carat. & my sinuses keep

getting rearranged by the Sturm und Drang
of the deli sauerkraut. Even the vitamin nook—

with its bottles full of capsules full of alchemized
optimism—sports a preteen blush. & beside that, the Arts

& Crafts corner promises genuine folk. Camelhair
rocking chairs, splotched oilcloths, tastefully distressed

garden trowels. & the centerpiece: a fraying duvet
lolled over milk crates. Above it, a woodcut that reads *Authentic*

Appalachian Coverlet—Stitched by Yesterday's
People. & in tinier font: *From Their Knobby*

Loom to Your Drawing Room. But the tag tells me smug
almost that it was devised in Delaware, woven

in Pakistan. I can't account for why, but my pupils just went
to pieces. Like old aspirin. Crying

kosher salt, I start to unburden
my buggy: toss the probiotic, the pulsated micro

greens. Piss off to the flax seed, the ethical cashew
goo. In slow hurry, I say *today, I'm spryer*

than I've ever been, & step deluxe to the ice
chest. In fine fettle, all fast-twitch brawn, I check out with zero

beyond the trailblazer essentials: meal, headcheese, corn
swill. Quinine & a coonskin. The cashier shoots me

a schoolmarm look, & I say *lady, all I need
is something that'll prefab a turd.* "Triumph"

by the venerable Bradford Paisley is loosed
from the loudspeaker. A suckling contrarian, I steeltoe

through the automatic doors. Outside, southwesternest
Connecticut. The first hoary *ahems* of fall

in the Cash Belt. Truly, this soothsaid chill tries its best
to teethe on me. Never fear: I'm wearing a windcheater

the color of buzzards circling
back south.

Thanks-Giving

It comes at & at you, this life. There's no white flag for it.
        Too often, your cheeks are sandblasted
from weeping, high thespian breaths. You smother in the crazy

quilt of mood. & it's blood-kin
        to bronchitis, something cinching you
witless. Times, just nailing one minute to the next

is carpentry. But right now I am put together. My nerves
        are unstrummed & don't do
what they shouldn't. Hell, it's almost creaturely in here

in this house that's evermore triaged me & mine.
        The curtains are black
cascades of Hefty Bag. There is a harlequin telenovella going

scraggly on VHS. & in the kitchen they are playing Rook
        by pilot light. Across from me
in this sawdust parlor is a casket

girthy as a Studebaker. What we are doing
        is what the warpainted
Picts would call sitting up with the dead. On the midget pillow

is my distant cousin, his brow damask with formaldehyde. He lived
        a life long & sour enough to see his kids all develop

allergies to him. His namesake told me what he remembered
        from childhood was the old man's black boots
by the front door looking like discipline.

Behind his back they called him Herr Papa. None of them
        wanted to stay up & see him on. So we are

ferrying the poleboat in a pinch. We couldn't afford to have him
  whole-hog embalmed, & the heat has curdled his showing
parts—even the thermostat is tearing up

quicksilver from the zap of it—but still I pay my respects. I see his lips
  drawn tart as wormwood. In life,
that mouth was a slum. Section 8 for acid sentiment. & as

above, so below. I drape my palm across his brisket,
  Kevlar-strict, in benediction. There is fanfare

from the kitchen; someone's played the Rook. Stepping out,
  the porchboards grouse like a mamaw with fibromyalgia.
Centuries & they still can't get comfortable. I can't

deny that death is lodging here—one shiver of the nostril could
  hunch it out—& I can't deny that plowboy hands & cuticles

of pig-iron laid our hearthstone. That in the millennium past
  all we've managed to do is swap crowbait mules
for croupy S-10s. & for all our pathfinders & men

who are plum-center with a rifle, we haven't the vaguest
  bede on progress. But, nights like this—tire-fires mellowed
to ember in each yard: the tint

& timbre of fawns bedding down—I've the gumption to look square
  in the face my hardships & say *you aren't*

as many as you were. Nights like this, even I'd have to admit
  that I only live a few hollers from tolerable

    if you put the thumbscrews to me.

Acknowledgments

Many thanks to the editors of the following publications, where poems in this collection first appeared (often in different versions):

American Literary Review: "Love in the Time of Company Towns"
Anodyne Magazine (Germany): "Hormonal"
Appalachian Journal: "Pilgrim" and "After Breakfast, Knott County, 2007"
Appalachian Places: "Every Day is Like Sunday" and "Psalm to Be Spoken Inside a Hill's Ribcage, Where the Heart Ought Be"
Arts & Letters: "Thanks-Giving" and "If I Know Me"
Barrelhouse Magazine: "Elegy for JOANN Fabrics"
Broad River Review: "Foxfire"
Cherry Tree: "Pitching Fits"
Cider Press Review: "A Day Laborer Dreams Away His Drive Home"
Connecticut River Review: "A Country Horse-Doctor"
Cutleaf: "Rite"
Delta Poetry Review: "The Collected Works of Judas Iscariot" and "Diatribe of the Runner-Up in a Piddling Local Election"
Floyd County Moonshine: "Rough Customer"
Grist: "Hormonal"
Jelly Bucket: "All Assurances, This was South"
Kentucky Monthly Magazine: "Injury to Insult"
Leavings Literary Magazine: "Nightwatchmen"
Mississippi Review: "Aesthete"
Narrative Magazine: "Sleep Apnea" and "Parts & Labor"
New Limestone Review: "Pure Fool"
Painted Bride Quarterly: "Bellyaching"
Pembroke Magazine: "Blue Yodel for Back When" and "37.4029° N, 82.8063° W"
Pine Mountain Sand & Gravel: An Appalachian Anthology: "Rough Customer"
Poetry Northwest: "Nocturne for August, Ailing Things"

Redivider: "Those Old Chromosomes Were Known to Ramble"
River Heron Review: "Zeitgeist & Gristle"
Reed Magazine: "We Were Put on This Earth to Fart Around"
Rock & Sling: "Pastoral vs. Georgic"
Shawangunk Review: "Sonnet for the Preachiest Loop in My Belt"
South Florida Poetry Journal: "We Still Kill the Old Way"
South 85 Journal: "Codependents"
Still: The Journal: "Crowfare"
storySouth: "Say Wise Things or Die, Egghead"
The Journal: "Visiting the Barn the Night Before I Burn it Down"
the minnesota review: "Cost of Living"
The Penn Review: "Otherlight"
The Swannanoa Review: "Crowbarring into a Schoolhouse at an Obscene Hour"
The Tomahawk Creek Review: "Sons of Perdition, KY"
Tar River Poetry: "Recoil"

Personal Thanks

This book would have never materialized without the sustained love and support of countless people. A few merit special thanks: my precious wife, Emaly; my father, Charles David; my mother, Cindy; and my sisters, Katie and Tara. They are and have always been my bedrock.

I owe so very much to the rest of my family as well. I want to list all my aunts, uncles, and cousins in individuated detail because each one of them has, in their own singular way, left an indelible imprint on me and my worldview. But, for fear of this devolving into one of those "Goodnight..." scenes from *The Waltons,* I will have to thank them collectively. My undying love and loyalty to the Hall family. It fills me with the utmost pride to declare that I am one of you forever.

Thanks also to the trusted friends, writers, and thinkers who have helped this book (and me myself) along at crucial stages: Ryan Lee, Jared Slayden, A.P. Walton, Max Lasky, and Forrest Rapier.

And, finally, my sincerest gratitude to James Kimbrell and Stephen Hundley, who helped shepherd these poems, and this collection as a whole, from infancy to maturity.

ABOUT THE AUTHOR

Ian Hall was born and reared in the coalfields of Southeastern Kentucky. He holds an MFA from the University of Tennessee, Knoxville, and he is currently a PhD candidate in English at Florida State University. He appeared on *Narrative Magazine*'s '30 Below 30' list, and he was named the winner of the 2025 Princemere Poetry Prize, as well as the co-winner of the Kentucky State Poetry Society's 2025 Grand Prix Contest, and the runner-up of the 2025 Vivian Shipley Poetry Award. He was named a finalist for the 2024 X.J. Kennedy Prize, the 2024 Tennessee Williams Poetry Prize, and the 2025 Red Wheelbarrow Poetry Prize. His work is featured in numerous publications, including *Narrative, Mississippi Review, The Journal,* and *American Literary Review.* He lives in Tallahassee, Florida.

www.ingramcontent.com/pod-product-compliance
Lightning Source LLC
LaVergne TN
LVHW011047100526
838202LV00078B/3753